The Cocktail Book

A MACDONALD BOOK

First published in Great Britain in 1983
by Macdonald & Co (Publishers) Ltd
London & Sydney

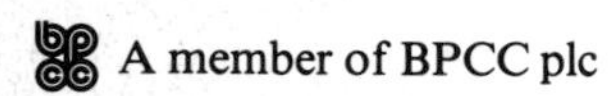
A member of BPCC plc

ISBN 0 356 09796 X

Printed and bound
in Italy

Macdonald & Co (Publishers) Ltd
Maxwell House
74 Worship Street
London EC2A 2EN

Cover photograph: Ray Massey
Cover design: Richard Johnson

The Cocktail Book

Gino Marcialis and
Franco Zingales

English translation by
Alison Grant

MACDONALD & CO
LONDON & SYDNEY

List of cocktails

Contents

The world in a glass

1

The world in a glass

Cocktail: what a strange word, full of mystery and fascination. Let us think about it for a moment, and try to discover its origins, its secrets, and the reason for its success.

All over Europe, the popularity of cocktails spread rapidly after the end of the Second World War, thanks to the influence of the Americans who, in the same way as the French troops under Napoleon, permanently influenced the customs and habits of the people in the countries in which they were based.

Of course, we also have to consider the ever-present influence of the specialists such as barmen, who understand not only all the secrets of mixing and blending, but also the inspiration of a fleeting, magical moment. That special moment, timeless and unforeseen, which witnesses the creation of an exciting new drink: a process in which imagination, personality and experience all combine with the demands of the exacting customer from Manhattan or Regent Street, the Via Veneto or the Côte d'Azur. The repertoire of cocktails is constantly expanding as these moments of inspiration take place in the celebrated bars of Acapulco, Bangkok and Cortina d'Ampezzo, in nightclubs, and in such international meeting places as the Ritz in Paris, the Rosati in Rome, the Waldorf Astoria in New York, Harry's Bar in Rome or Venice and luxury hotels all over the world. The number of lounge-bars in transatlantic liners and cruise-ships bound for the Caribbean is forever growing, and life on board lends itself very well to pleasant encounters and moments of relaxation over an aperitif or an exotic cocktail. And it is in situations such as this that exotic new cocktails are often created, many with mysterious-sounding names which delight the ear. Little by little, given the right circumstances, the drink will become widely-known, and in some special cases (where the inventor or the first person to try it is an artist, a poet, or a famous politician, for example) it will achieve international renown and become a public favourite.

What is a cocktail? The American magazine *The Balance* in its issue of May 1806 gave the following definition: 'A cocktail is an intoxicating beverage composed of different spirits, which, mixed with bitters and essences produce an outstanding drink.' The *Nouveau Petit Larousse* has the following entry under cocktail: '*mélange de boissons alcooliques, de sirop et de glace*', while the *Nuovo Dizionario Spagnolo* (Ambruzzi) has an entry under *coctel* which bestows the label of 'garish apéritif' on it, an unusual description of its qualities of synthesis and expression. It is also worth mentioning the definition given in the *Merriam-Webster Dictionary* in 1971: 'a short, iced drink containing a strong alcoholic base (as rum, whiskey or gin) or occasionally wine, with the mixture either by stirring or shaking of flavoring and sometimes coloring ingredients (as fruit juice, egg, bitters, liqueurs or sugar) and often garnished (as with a sprig of mint or slice of lemon).' Another dictionary (*The American Heritage Dictionary of the English Language*) defines a cocktail thus: 'Any of various mixed alcoholic drinks, often served chilled, consisting usually of brandy, whiskey or gin combined with fruit juices or other liqueurs.'

The history of man and that of alcoholic beverages have always proceeded along parallel lines for as far back as we know. Primitive man turned to alcohol, having stumbled upon the fermentation of the juices and pulp of different fruits, starch and other substances, believing that he would find in these early ingredients a powerful force which would sustain him in a life beset with tribulations. He had, therefore, already set out on the long search for a magical formula, an elixir, which was to lead him through many obstacles and much delusion.

The story is the same whether we look at the Egyptians, the Chinese, the Aztecs, the Indians, or the natives of Yukatan (Mexico) who, according to legend, invented a concoction, the contents of which are not really known, but for which they used a kind of spoon carved out of the roots of a plant known as the cocktail. Gabrielli's dictionary can help us a little here, but even he is really in the dark, claiming, however, that the origin of the word is in doubt: 'most people divide the word into its two components *cock* and *tail*, and regard it as having come from American slang, but nobody really understands the connection between the tail of a cock and a drink'.

Some people claim that cocktails originated in Italy. Pierre Andrieu, one of the most authoritative French cookery experts, recalled in the publication *Industrie Hôtelière* how the Italians who came to France with Catherine de Medici's household in the seventeenth century brought with them the custom of mixing different alcoholic drinks. 'It would take a whole chapter to describe the drinks,' wrote Andrieu. 'Thanks to the Florentine courtiers, the use of ratafia and cherry brandy spread. We are told that the ministers of the time would toast the signing of acts and agreements with the words *"Ut rata fiat"*.' In 1604, the French minister Sully claimed that among the unnecessary expenditure made by French people was that incurred by feasting and drinking.

In his book *Life in Paris under Louis XII* Louis Battifol wrote that for a long time the only liqueur consumed in France was moscato from Spain, ippocrasso (a sort of mulled wine) and mead. When vinegar merchants began to distil brandy they had the idea of selling cherries conserved in brandy and served in small glasses or cups. Brandy thus sweetened with sugar or fruit was called 'eau clairette'. Italians who came to France in the seventeenth century in Catherine de Medici's household – to refer once more to Andrieu's article – began to replace the cherries with lemons, oranges, strawberries, blackcurrants, raspberries and apricots. In this way the first liqueurs flavoured with different fruits appeared. No restrictions were imposed upon the sale of these liqueurs until the reign of Louis XIV, the Sun King, who set up the society of lemonade merchants, uniting them with the brandy distillers in 1676.

'We therefore recognize in Catherine de Medici,' Andrieu goes on, 'the figure who introduced cocktails to France.' From there they soon reached England, and it was not long before they also reached her colonies, which then included the area that is now the United States of America. From there these drinks have returned to England in a different guise.

The names of the famous turn up at regular intervals in the history of cocktails. One such figure is the writer Ernest Hemingway, who emphasized the pleasure of a life punctuated by plenty of good wine and short drinks enjoyed in a friendly atmosphere, often shared with illustrious friends, writers, artists, politicians and scientists from all over the world. There was a time when celebrities, including royalty, frequented the peaceful bars of the grand hotels and the glittering salons of the fashionable cafés. Conversation and discussions about topical issues provided interest and entertainment in the company of friends, and often a cocktail would help create a convivial atmosphere. Thus drinks which later became known all over the world were first created.

Some names which are now famous, such as Negroni, were created on the spur of the moment. The original recipe, served at the Casoni bar in Florence, a fashionable rendezvous in 1919, was made with a base of red Cinzano vermouth to which Campari was added. This was the classic Americano, but count Camillo Negroni, a regular customer, introduced the idea of adding a little gin, so that the barman, Fosco Scarselli, was forever being asked for the drink 'as Count Negroni has it'. From there it was easy to rename the cocktail, which is now drunk everywhere. Other drinks which are famous throughout the world are Bloody Mary, (named after Mary Pickford, the unforgettable actress of the thirties), and Caruso (dedicated to the tenor who won the heart of the American nation).

The experts

There used to be an international circle whose centre of attraction was a barman of the old school, the sort who lived only for his work, who created sophisticated cocktails, and drew inspiration from the fine features of a well-born lady, from the scowling face of a politician and from the absent look of a financial or industrial tycoon. Many of these cocktails, with a renown that was often ephemeral because they were too closely bound to a particular fleeting moment in history or legend, have involved the best barmen of the world in a competition which is not generally known about because, despite contact with a very mixed, demanding international clientele (a contact which enabled the barmen to acquire knowledge and experience), the barmen have maintained a dignified professional silence. Under these circumstances it is clear that, to be a lasting success, the cocktail depends on a well-informed choice of liqueur mixers and flavourings, and preferably high-quality brands (to use others is false economy). Its impact hinges on careful preparation with accurate measurement of the various ingredients, otherwise a blend of liqueurs becomes an undrinkable mixture. The smell is also important, as is the 'texture' (not to be confused with the density) which is the result of the synthesis of the various ingredients, and is the mark of the personality both of the cocktail and its inventor.

The French author J. K. Huysmans (1848–1907), renowned for his great aesthetic sensitivity, wrote a novel called *A Rebours*, the heroine of which is a woman called Floressas des Esseintes. Tired of the monotony and mediocrity of her surroundings, she decides to retire to a house in the country inhabited only by fantastic dreams and phials containing exotic perfumes made from complex and mysterious formulae.

A special container fitted with numerous valves allows her to mix several different liquids together in a small silver bottle. Madame des Esseintes sips a few drops and immediately she feels symphonies inside herself which have the same effect as music does upon the ear, because, seen through her fertile imagination – already drawn towards a world of dreams and shadows – the taste of each liquid corresponds to the sound of a musical instrument. In this way curaçao, for example, resembles the velvety sound of the clarinet, mint and aniseed can be compared to the flute, while gin and whisky recall the trombone. Madame des Esseintes goes on to imagine how all these instruments could be orchestrated – a quintet, perhaps, with the violin representing vintage brandy, the viola rum, the 'cello vodka, and the double bass vermouth. She is carried away by a tide of ecstasy until she has imagined a complete magical concerto.

In everyday life, the general desire for a pleasing sense of euphoria is met by the large number of premises designed for the consumption of alcohol. The number of American bars, English pubs, well-stocked traditional Continental bars, drinks-bars, bars in well-known hotels, night-clubs and private clubs has increased to meet the same need. In bars today barmen will prepare with apparent ease cocktails for the customer to try. This off-hand manner provokes varying reactions; some people are filled with admiration, others smile scornfully at the elaborate (but necessary) mixing in the shaker.

There is no doubt that it is easy to heap criticism and scorn on the way drinks have come to be used as a social habit, but let us consider also the heights of perfection and quality which have been attained. The details of the early production of alcoholic drinks have been lost in the mist of time. It took centuries of experimenting before the first still was invented – as far back as the third century AD Greek alchemists in Alexandria were working to solve the problem of the dispersal of the value of distillation. The Romans, the Greeks and the peoples of those countries now known as the Middle East enjoyed aromatic wines such as *absinthiatum*, from which vermouth derives, or *vinum hippocraticum*, a sort of mead much favoured at the court of Louis XIV and Louis XV, which was made by adding almonds, cinnamon and honey to the wine for sweetness. The Camaldolesi monks of the order of Brother Romualdo invented a recipe which is impressive in its simplicity (brandy and plum juice) and which was believed at the time to be a protection against malaria.

This brings us up to around AD 1000. From there one development follows another until the present day. This progress has been recorded in various studies, and in particular in those made by Jean Baptiste Van Helmont and Van Leeuwenhaek in the seventeenth century who wrote about the phenomenon of fermentation. In the eighteenth century A. Laurent Lavoisier concentrated on the transformation, caused by the yeast, of the sugary content of grapes into alcohol and carbon dioxide. Let us remember, too, Guy Lussac and Louis Pasteur who, by taking further the discoveries already made by other scientists, discovered the fundamental rules of distillation.

The last few centuries have witnessed the rise of some of the most famous and prestigious names in the alcohol industry such as Bols (1580), Martell (1715), Drioli di Zara (1738), Cinzano (1757), Hennessy (1765), Coral (1802), Buton (1820), Luxardo (1821), Florio (1832), Martini (1840), Branca (1848), Distillers Corporation Seagrams (1868), Stock (1884). All these firms, and others just as worthy of mention, have contributed with their products towards the development of alcoholic concoctions, from the simplest to the most elaborate, which have been made all over the world, and served at cocktail parties to the most illustrious figures.

The tricks of the trade

It is for the customer that cocktails are created; to please him, and to satisfy his often subconscious wishes. It is here that the barman comes into his own: formal and dignified, in his distinctive jacket, and yet at the same time casual, he goes about making the cocktail he has chosen or created on the spur of the moment to suit the new customer who is standing expectantly before him, and whom he has immediately and intuitively summed up with one expert glance.

It is not without a touch of

psychology that he categorizes his customers after a brief but penetrating examination; they could be members of high society, industrialists, trade representatives, businessmen from abroad, young romantics, or simply 'regulars'. But, we may well ask, how do barmen manage to classify the indistinguishable hordes of people who pass before their eyes like so many robots? The barman is very alert to small clues. Perhaps he will notice a distinctive tie or small badge which will tell him what the profession, special interest or club of his customer is. Or the game might be given away by the customer who remembers and repeats a previous conversation, which happened to have taken place at a smart hotel in Rome, or Paris, or London.

There can only be one explanation for the unique regard in which barmen are held; it is the fruit of years of study and quiet observation. For it must be said that the role of the barman is not easily learnt, and requires, on the contrary, a long and difficult apprenticeship. The beginner first observes the expert, then tries to emulate him, and is by this stage often carried away by the desire to enter the various competitions (first on a local level, then national, and eventually even international).

All this will enrich the experience of the barman and may lead him towards ever loftier goals all over the world in the name of professionalism. For one of the roles of the barman is to educate public taste (cocktails cannot be improvised) and to refine it according to certain fixed rules, which emphasize the importance of high-quality well-chosen ingredients, accurate measures and suitable accompaniments. It is a difficult art, and those who succeed in making it their vocation have to be prepared to make large sacrifices.

And what about the customer? Well, if he also understands the meaning of real contact with his cocktail he will certainly know how to choose his own barman, to whom he will confide all his troubles, and whom he knows he can rely upon to produce a delightful cocktail with an allusive magical name which will be guaranteed to obliviate all his cares. Choosing a name for a new drink is a very delicate art, and has a lot to do with its success or failure. Cocktails are given every possible sort of name, from the simplest to the most unusual, from the most ordinary to the most pretentious.

The latter is true particularly in the case of entries to the various competitions, when beginners, throwing respect and trepidation to the winds, compete against the old hands of the profession. Whether refined, romantic, philosophical or malicious, a quick delicate flick in the shaker confers on these names an elevated tone which qualifies them for entry in national and international events. These names, sometimes spontaneous, sometimes the result of careful thought or observation of a particular social or family environment, take off to make their way in the world.

Let us spare a thought for the

very difficult task of the official tasters and the judges (carefully chosen for their expertise and knowledge) who have, with traditional impartiality, to choose, to reject one in favour of another. Of course, the entries in a competition have to remain anonymous. The judges carry out their work of tasting seriously and silently, concentrating hard, and using their senses of smell and taste to the utmost to guide them in their search. These men are respected for their sensitivity and as representatives of an age-old tradition; the competitions and judging are solemn rites, characterized by good taste, elegance and fair play. When all is said and done, it is a wearisome process for the creator, seeking to pin down carefully those indefinable characteristics which are the hallmark of the successful cocktail. There are inevitably moments of trepidation, of anxiety, and, if things do not turn out as expected, of disappointment and temporary discouragement. However, as the saying goes, the important thing is not to win but to participate, and both winners and losers can claim credit for having made possible a fair competition where experience, training and inspiration can find expression.

It is worth sparing a few words at this point for the aspect of the cocktail which makes the first impression upon the crowds of enthusiasts for this 'sport' of drinking and that is its appearance. This is a particularly important feature in the case of long drinks. Gin, vermouth, vodka, brandy, rum, kummel, whisky, and the various other spirits which require complicated distillation as well as fruit juices and liqueurs, are without doubt the most important substances used. These can be toned down or livened up as required with an egg white or a drop of grenadine or other syrup. By combining these classic ingredients in the shaker, a mixture is obtained whose colour may be ruby-red, crimson, amber, deep yellow or paler yellow, but which will always be *personal* and inviting. Of course, although it is to the eye that the first appeal is made, it is with the taste buds that the subtle nuances of the drink are appreciated, the hidden flavours and the delicate blending which, if done with great accuracy, give rise to that feeling of well-being which in turn establishes or confirms the reputation of the inventor.

Once released, from the shaker, where the correct hue and consistency have been achieved, the cocktail is poured into a suitable glass and adorned with exotic and original decorations. In the case of a long drink, these might consist of a mini Chinese sunshade, a red cherry on a cocktail stick surrounded by a ruff of orange, or pineapple cut in cubes. All these may be balanced on the rim of the glass, and can give an overall impression of the cubist style, or the dadaist, or baroque, or may simply be the result of the individual imagination, perhaps futuristic. The success of a cocktail will always depend to a certain degree upon its presentation, because it is an indication of the barman's style and ability. The customer-judge who stares intently at the glass placed in front of him is often spell-bound by what he sees.

Special occasions

It is possible to recreate the atmosphere of a good cocktail bar at home. With a minimal supply of well-chosen drinks (red and white vermouth, gin, whisky, vodka, grappa, brandy, rum, angostura bitters), the bar becomes a focal point where friends and acquaintances can be invited for light and pleasant conversation or the discussion of current affairs. A bar provides a convivial atmosphere where one can relax over a cocktail and enjoy the company of others. Often one person takes the lead in making conversation, first equipping himself with a full glass, even if he feels it necessary to excuse the fact with the words of St. Bernard of Chiaravalle, who said, in the course of an excellent meal prepared for a group of pilgrims: 'It is not I who have eaten and drunk, it is my hospitality.' Once a bar has been set up at home, it can provide a focal point for all kinds of get-togethers – special occasions such as anniversaries, weddings or engagements, promotions, house-warmings, business meetings, or to celebrate the arrival or departure of friends or to socialize with people from work.

The atmosphere at a cocktail party is often quite special (the Americans are very good at achieving this), yet it need not be expensive or time-consuming to hold one, especially if sangria or cups (prepared slightly in advance) are among the drinks chosen to be served. Usually a successful cocktail will provoke curiosity amongst the guests about its preparation. It is then up to the host or hostess, who is acting as barman, to explain in simple terms the reasons for their choice of drinks being served. It may be because of a pleasant discovery they have made, or because they have heard friends singing the praises of a certain cocktail, or else they may have simply tried out a recipe they saw in a newspaper or book, or heard on the radio or television. It can be fun to christen a new cocktail, perhaps by having an impromptu friendly competition, or naming the drink after one of the people present or a mutual happy memory.

So, the world of the cocktail is a very colourful one which is at the same time both old and new. A different way of drinking, and one to be taken up by those who enjoy friendship and companionship.

When the recipe calls for a twist of peel to be used, a little of the oil or zest of the fruit is introduced into the cocktail by twisting the peel over the surface of the drink before adding it to the cocktail.

Some cocktails stand out among the innumerable recipes, and are known all over the world; these are the fifty cocktails laid down by the members of the International Bartenders Association, the only international organization for barmen. How to make these fifty 'international' cocktails is described in the following pages. Under each heading the original IBA recipe is given first, with the proportions of each ingredient expressed as fractions, while the quantities are left to the maker's choice. Alongside is a recipe adapted by Gino Marcialis for the non-expert which uses dessertspoons (with a capacity of approximately 10–15 ml) as the main measure.

50 international cocktails

2

1. Adonis

2/3 dry sherry
1/3 red vermouth
1 dash orange bitters
1 twist orange peel

Prepare in a mixing glass.

4–5 ice cubes
4 spoons dry sherry
2 spoons red vermouth
1 dash orange bitters
1 twist orange peel

Place the ice in a large mixing glass, and pour in the other ingredients in the order listed above. Stir with a special stirrer or a long-handled spoon. To serve, pour into a cocktail glass, removing the ice with a strainer. Add the twist of orange peel.

Adonis

2. *Affinity*

½ Scotch whisky
¼ dry vermouth
¼ red vermouth
2 dashes Angostura bitters

Prepare in a mixing glass.

4–5 ice cubes
3 spoons Scotch whisky
1½ spoons dry vermouth
1½ spoons red vermouth
1 dash Angostura bitters

Place the ice cubes in the mixing glass, pour in the other ingredients in the order listed above, and stir with a long-handled spoon. To serve, pour into a cocktail glass, removing the ice with a strainer.

Affinity

3. Alaska

$\frac{3}{4}$ gin
$\frac{1}{4}$ yellow Chartreuse

Prepare in a shaker with crushed ice.

4–5 ice cubes
1 spoon gin
1 spoon yellow Chartreuse

Place the ice in the shaker, pour in the gin and the Chartreuse and shake for a few seconds. Serve in a cocktail glass.

Alaska

4. Alexander

$\frac{1}{3}$ cognac
$\frac{1}{3}$ crème de cacao
$\frac{1}{3}$ fresh cream

Prepare in a shaker with crushed ice, taking care that the drink is shaken well.

4–5 ice cubes
2 spoons cognac
2 spoons crème de cacao
2 spoons fresh cream
1 pinch grated nutmeg

Place all the ingredients in the shaker except the nutmeg and shake vigorously for a few moments. Serve in a large cocktail glass or open-style champagne glass, sprinkling the nutmeg on top of the drink.

Alexander

5.

Angel face

1/3 dry gin
1/3 apricot brandy
1/3 calvados

Prepare in a shaker.

4–5 ice cubes
2 spoons dry gin
2 spoons apricot brandy
2 spoons calvados

Place the ice in the shaker, add the other ingredients and shake vigorously for a few moments. Serve in a cocktail glass.

Angel face

6. Bacardi

$\frac{2}{3}$ white rum
$\frac{1}{3}$ lemon juice
1 dash grenadine

Prepare in a shaker with crushed ice.

4–5 ice cubes
4 spoons white rum
1 dash grenadine
2 spoons lemon juice

Prepare in a shaker, adding first the ice, then the rum, the grenadine and the strained, freshly-squeezed lemon juice. Shake well for a few seconds and pour into a large cocktail glass or an open-style champagne glass. In some parts of South America and the Caribbean (especially Cuba) this cocktail is made with green lime juice.

Bacardi

7. Bamboo

½ dry sherry
½ dry vermouth
1 dash orange bitters

Prepare in a mixing glass.

4–5 ice cubes
3 spoons dry sherry
3 spoons dry vermouth
1 dash orange bitters
1 twist lemon peel

Cool the mixing glass with the ice cubes. Strain the ice cubes, returning them to the glass and throwing away any water. This step in this little-known drink is most important. Then pour in the ingredients, stir for a few seconds and serve in a cocktail glass with the twist of lemon.

Bamboo

8. Bentley

$\frac{1}{2}$ *calvados*
$\frac{1}{2}$ *Dubonnet*

Prepare in a shaker with crushed ice.

4–5 ice cubes
3 spoons calvados
3 spoons Dubonnet

Place the ice in the shaker, add the calvados and the Dubonnet and shake for a few seconds before pouring into a cocktail glass. This is a little-known cocktail.

Bentley

9. Between the sheets

$\frac{1}{3}$ white rum
$\frac{1}{3}$ Cointreau
$\frac{1}{3}$ brandy
1 dash lemon juice

Prepare in a shaker with a little crushed ice.

4–5 ice cubes
2 spoons white rum
2 spoons Cointreau
2 spoons brandy
juice of $\frac{1}{2}$ lemon

Place the ingredients in the shaker in the order above. Shake for a few seconds and serve in a large cocktail glass.

Between the sheets

10. Block and fall

$\frac{1}{3}$ cognac
$\frac{1}{3}$ Cointreau
$\frac{1}{6}$ calvados
$\frac{1}{6}$ anisette

Prepare by stirring together.

4–5 ice cubes
2 spoons cognac
2 spoons Cointreau
1 spoon calvados
1 spoon Pernod

Place the ice in the shaker then add the other ingredients in the order given above. Shake for a few seconds and serve in a cocktail glass.

Block and fall

11. Bloody Mary

⅖ iced vodka
2 dashes Worcestershire sauce
⅗ iced tomato juice
1 dash lemon juice

Prepare directly in a tumbler, stirring well with a suitable spoon. Add celery salt, Tabasco and pepper to taste.

3 spoons tomato juice
salt or celery salt
pepper or a few dashes Tabasco sauce
1 dash lemon juice
1 or 2 dashes Worcestershire sauce
2 spoons iced vodka

Pour the tomato juice into a medium-sized tumbler, add the desired seasoning, the freshly-squeezed lemon juice and the Worcestershire sauce. Stir well. Finally add the vodka, stir again briefly and serve.

Bloody Mary

12. *Bobby Burns*

½ Scotch whisky
½ red vermouth
3 dashes Bénédictine

Prepare in a mixing glass.

4–5 ice cubes
3 spoons Scotch whisky
3 spoons red vermouth
1 dash Bénédictine
1 twist lemon peel

Cool the mixing glass with the ice cubes. Strain the ice cubes, returning them to the glass and throwing away any water. Pour in the whisky, vermouth and Bénédictine. Stir with a long-handled spoon. Serve in a cocktail glass, with the twist of lemon peel.

Bobby Burns

Ballantine's
ESTABLISHED 1827
QUALITY GUARANTEED
40°
FINEST
PRODUCT OF SCOTLAND

13. Bombay

½ brandy
¼ dry vermouth
¼ red vermouth
1 dash pastis
2 dashes curaçao

Prepare by stirring together with a little crushed ice.

4–5 ice cubes
3 spoons brandy
1½ spoons dry vermouth
1½ spoons red vermouth
1 dash pastis
2 dashes curaçao

Place the ice cubes in the shaker, then add the brandy, the vermouths, the pastis and the curaçao. Shake for a few seconds and serve in a cocktail glass.

Bombay

14. Bronx

$\frac{1}{2}$ dry gin
$\frac{1}{6}$ orange juice
$\frac{1}{6}$ dry vermouth
$\frac{1}{6}$ red vermouth

Prepare in a shaker with a little crushed ice.

4–5 ice cubes
2 spoons dry gin
1 spoon dry vermouth
1 spoon red vermouth
2 spoons orange juice

Place the ice in the shaker, add the gin, the vermouth and the freshly-squeezed orange juice and shake vigorously for a few seconds. Serve in a large cocktail glass or an open-style champagne glass.

Bronx

15. Brooklyn

$\frac{2}{3}$ rye whiskey
$\frac{1}{3}$ red vermouth
1 dash maraschino
1 dash Amer Picon

Prepare in a mixing glass with a little crushed ice, stirring well.

4–5 ice cubes
4 spoons rye whiskey
2 spoons red vermouth
$\frac{1}{2}$ teaspoon maraschino
$\frac{1}{2}$ teaspoon Amer Picon

Place the ice in a mixing glass, add the other ingredients and stir for a few seconds. Serve in a cocktail glass.

Brooklyn

16. Caruso

$\frac{1}{3}$ dry gin
$\frac{1}{3}$ dry vermouth
$\frac{1}{3}$ green crème de menthe

Prepare by stirring together with a little crushed ice.

4–5 ice cubes
2 spoons dry gin
2 spoons dry vermouth
2 spoons green crème de menthe

Place the ice cubes in the shaker and pour in the gin, the vermouth and the crème de menthe. Shake for a few seconds and serve in a cocktail glass.

Caruso

17. Casino

$\frac{9}{12}$ dry gin
$\frac{1}{12}$ maraschino
$\frac{1}{12}$ dash orange bitters
$\frac{1}{12}$ lemon juice

Prepare in a shaker with a little crushed ice. Serve in a cocktail glass and decorate with a cherry.

4–5 ice cubes
4 spoons dry gin
$\frac{1}{2}$ spoon maraschino
$\frac{1}{2}$ spoon orange juice
$\frac{1}{2}$ spoon lemon juice
1 maraschino cherry

Place the ice in the shaker, then add the other ingredients in the order given above (except the cherry, which is for decoration). Shake for a few seconds and serve in a cocktail glass.

Casino

18. Claridge

$\frac{1}{3}$ dry gin
$\frac{1}{3}$ dry vermouth
$\frac{1}{6}$ apricot brandy
$\frac{1}{6}$ Cointreau

Prepare in a mixing glass with a little crushed ice.

4–5 ice cubes
2 spoons dry gin
2 spoons dry vermouth
1 spoon apricot brandy
1 spoon Cointreau

Place the ice cubes in a mixing glass, then add the other ingredients in the order shown above. Stir with a long-handled spoon and serve in a cocktail glass.

Claridge

19. Clover club

$\frac{2}{3}$ dry gin
$\frac{1}{3}$ grenadine
juice $\frac{1}{2}$ lemon
$\frac{1}{2}$ egg white

Prepare in a shaker with a little crushed ice. Serve in a large cocktail glass.

4–5 ice cubes
4 spoons dry gin
2 spoons grenadine
juice $\frac{1}{2}$ lemon
$\frac{1}{2}$ egg white

Place the ice cubes and the other ingredients in the shaker. Shake for 8–10 seconds. Serve in a large cocktail glass or a wine goblet.

Clover club

20. Czarina

$\frac{1}{2}$ *vodka*
$\frac{1}{4}$ *dry vermouth*
$\frac{1}{4}$ *apricot brandy*
1 dash Angostura bitters

Prepare in a mixing glass with a little crushed ice.

4–5 ice cubes
2 spoons vodka
1 spoon dry vermouth
1 spoon apricot brandy
1 dash Angostura bitters

Place the ice in the mixing glass and add the ingredients. Stir for a few seconds and serve in a cocktail glass.

Czarina

21. Daiquiri

¾ white rum
¼ lemon juice
3 dashes sugar syrup

Prepare in a shaker with ice.

4–5 ice cubes
4 spoons white rum
1 spoon lemon juice
½ teaspoon sugar syrup

Place the ice in a shaker, add the other ingredients and shake vigorously for a few seconds. Serve in a large cocktail glass or an open-style champagne glass.

Daiquiri

22. *Derby*

55 ml (2 oz) dry gin
2 dashes peach bitters
2 sprigs fresh mint

Prepare in a shaker with a little crushed ice.

4–5 ice cubes
6 spoons dry gin
1 dash peach bitters
2 sprigs fresh mint

Place the ice in the shaker and add the gin and the peach bitters. Shake well for a few seconds and serve in a cocktail glass. Decorate with the sprigs of mint. Alternatively, this drink can be served with ice in a medium-sized tumbler.

23. Diki-diki

$\frac{2}{3}$ calvados
$\frac{1}{6}$ Swedish punch
$\frac{1}{6}$ grapefruit juice

Prepare in a shaker.

4–5 ice cubes
4 spoons calvados
1 spoon Swedish punch
1 spoon grapefruit juice

Place the ice cubes in the shaker and pour in the calvados, the Swedish punch and the freshly-squeezed, strained grapefruit juice. Shake for a few seconds and serve in a cocktail glass.

Diki-diki

24. Duchess

⅓ red vermouth
⅓ dry vermouth
⅓ pastis

Prepare in a mixing glass with a little crushed ice, stirring vigorously.

4–5 ice cubes
2 spoons red vermouth
2 spoons dry vermouth
2 spoons pastis

Place the ice in a large mixing glass, then pour in the three ingredients. Stir with a long-handled spoon for a few seconds . To serve, pour into a cocktail glass, removing the ice with a strainer.

Duchess

25. East-India

$\frac{3}{4}$ brandy
$\frac{1}{8}$ curaçao
$\frac{1}{8}$ orange juice
1 dash Angostura bitters

Prepare in a shaker with a little crushed ice. Add a maraschino cherry and lemon twist.

4–5 ice cubes
4 spoons brandy
1 spoon curaçao
1 spoon orange juice
1 maraschino cherry

Place the ice in the shaker, then add the brandy, the curaçao and the strained orange juice. Shake vigorously for a few seconds then pour the drink into a large cocktail glass or a wine goblet. Decorate with the cherry.

East-India

26. Gibson

$\frac{5}{6}$ *dry gin*
$\frac{1}{6}$ *dry vermouth*
1 cocktail onion

Prepare in a mixing glass. Decorate the serving glass with the cocktail onion.

4–5 ice cubes
5 spoons dry gin
1 spoon dry vermouth
1 cocktail onion

Place the ice cubes in the mixing glass. Add the gin and the vermouth. Stir for a few moments and serve in a cocktail glass, decorated with the onion.

Gibson

27. Gin and it

$\frac{1}{2}$ dry gin
$\frac{1}{2}$ red vermouth

Prepare directly in the glass in which the cocktail is to be served, using chilled gin and vermouth and stirring gently with a spoon.

3 spoons dry gin
3 spoons chilled red vermouth

Prepare directly in a glass which has been chilled by placing in the freezer for at least 10 minutes.

Gin and it

28. Grand slam

$\frac{1}{2}$ *Swedish punch*
$\frac{1}{4}$ *red vermouth*
$\frac{1}{4}$ *dry vermouth*

Prepare by stirring together with a little crushed ice.

4–5 ice cubes
3 spoons Swedish punch
1 spoon red vermouth
1 spoon dry vermouth

Place the ice, then the punch, then the vermouths in the shaker. Shake for a few seconds before pouring into a cocktail glass.

29. Grasshopper

1/3 green crème de menthe
1/3 white crème de cacao
1/3 fresh cream

Prepare in a shaker with a little crushed ice. Serve in a large cocktail glass.

4–5 ice cubes
2 spoons green crème de menthe
2 spoons white crème de cacao
2 spoons fresh cream

Place the ice in the shaker and add the ingredients in the order given above. Shake for a few seconds then pour into a goblet or large cocktail glass.

Grasshopper

30. Manhattan

$\frac{2}{3}$ Canadian whiskey
$\frac{1}{3}$ red vermouth
1 dash Angostura bitters
1 maraschino cherry

Prepare the drink in a mixing glass.

4–5 ice cubes
4 spoons Canadian whiskey
2 spoons red vermouth
1 dash Angostura bitters
1 maraschino cherry

Place the ice cubes in a mixing glass. Add the whiskey, the vermouth and the Angostura bitters. Stir for a few seconds and pour into a cocktail glass, removing the ice with a strainer. Decorate with the cherry.

Manhattan

31. Martini dry

$\frac{3}{4}$ dry gin
$\frac{1}{4}$ dry vermouth

Prepare in a mixing glass, stirring vigorously.

4–5 ice cubes
5 spoons dry gin
1 spoon dry vermouth
1 twist lemon peel

This famous cocktail, amongst the best-known and most widely-drunk, should be prepared in a mixing glass, preferably chilled, briefly stirring the gin and the vermouth with the ice. Serve in a cocktail glass, with the twist of lemon peel.

Martini dry

32. Martini sweet

$\frac{2}{3}$ dry gin
$\frac{1}{3}$ red vermouth

Prepare in a mixing glass with a little crushed ice.

4–5 ice cubes
4 spoons dry gin
2 spoons red vermouth

This drink is also prepared in a mixing glass, stirring the gin and the vermouth with the ice for a few seconds. Serve in a cocktail glass which has been well chilled in advance.

Martini sweet

33. Mary Pickford

½ white rum
½ natural pineapple juice
1 teaspoon grenadine
6 dashes maraschino

Prepare in a shaker, shaking vigorously with a little ice.

4–5 ice cubes
3 spoons white rum
3 spoons natural pineapple juice
1 teaspoon grenadine
1 teaspoon maraschino

Place the ice in the shaker and pour the other ingredients over it. Shake for a few seconds, then serve in a large cocktail glass or a wine goblet.

Mary Pickford

34. Mikado

40 ml ($1\frac{3}{4}$ oz) brandy
2 drops curaçao
2 drops crème de noyaux
2 drops orange curaçao
2 drops orgeat
2 drops Angostura bitters

Prepare in a shaker with a little crushed ice.

4–5 ice cubes
4 spoons brandy
1 dash Angostura bitters
1 teaspoon crème de noyaux
1 teaspoon barley water
1 teaspoon curaçao

Pour the ingredients into the shaker in the order given above. Close and shake vigorously for a few seconds. Serve in a chilled cocktail glass.

Mikado

35. Monkey gland

$\frac{3}{5}$ dry gin
$\frac{2}{5}$ orange juice
2 dashes grenadine
2 dashes pastis

Prepare in a shaker with a little crushed ice.

4–5 ice cubes
4 spoons dry gin
1 spoon orange juice
$\frac{1}{2}$ teaspoon grenadine
$\frac{1}{2}$ teaspoon pastis

Place the ice cubes in the shaker. Pour in the gin, the freshly-squeezed orange juice, the grenadine and the pastis. Shake vigorously for a few seconds and serve in a cocktail glass or a wine goblet.

Monkey gland

36. Negroni

$\frac{1}{3}$ red vermouth
$\frac{1}{3}$ Campari
$\frac{1}{3}$ dry gin

Pour the ingredients directly into a medium-sized tumbler and stir well. Add soda if desired.

4–5 small ice cubes
2 spoons dry gin
2 spoons Campari
2 spoons red vermouth
$\frac{1}{2}$ thin slice orange

This famous Italian cocktail is prepared directly in a medium-sized tumbler. Stir the ingredients together and decorate with the slice of orange.

Negroni

37. Old Fashioned

1 lump sugar on to which 2 dashes Angostura bitters have been poured
½ slice orange
½ slice lemon
1 maraschino cherry
3 ice cubes
1 large measure rye whiskey
1 dash chilled soda water

Prepare in an Old Fashioned glass.

1 sugar lump
2 dashes Angostura bitters
1 slice orange
1 slice lemon
1 dash soda water
3 ice cubes
5 spoons rye whiskey
2 maraschino cherries

In an Old Fashioned glass, place the sugar lump soaked in the Angostura bitters, the slices of orange and lemon and the soda water, and stir well. Add the ice and the whiskey, stir again and decorate with the cherry.

Old Fashioned

38. Old pal

$\frac{1}{3}$ *rye whiskey*
$\frac{1}{3}$ *dry vermouth*
$\frac{1}{3}$ *Campari*

Prepare in a mixing glass.

4–5 ice cubes
2 spoons rye whiskey
2 spoons dry vermouth
2 spoons Campari

Place the ice cubes in the mixing glass. Add the whiskey, the vermouth and the Campari and stir for a few seconds. Serve in a chilled cocktail glass.

Old pal

39. Orange blossom

½ dry gin
½ orange juice

Prepare in a shaker.

4–5 ice cubes
4 spoons dry gin
4 spoons orange juice

Place the ice in a shaker. Pour in the strained orange juice and add the gin (with a teaspoon of sugar syrup if the oranges are bitter). Shake well for a few seconds and serve in a large cocktail glass or a wine glass.

Orange blossom

40. Oriental

$\frac{2}{4}$ *rye whiskey*
$\frac{1}{4}$ *red vermouth*
$\frac{1}{4}$ *white curaçao*
2 *teaspoons fresh lemon juice*

Prepare in a shaker with a little crushed ice.

4–5 *ice cubes*
2 *spoons rye whiskey*
1 *spoon red vermouth*
1 *spoon white curaçao*
1 *spoon lemon juice*

This cocktail should be shaken vigorously for a few seconds, and if it is to be served *on the rocks* a medium-sized tumbler should be used. Otherwise, serve in a large cocktail glass.

Oriental

41. Paradise

½ dry gin
¼ apricot brandy
¼ orange juice

Prepare in a shaker with crushed ice.

4–5 ice cubes
3 spoons dry gin
½ spoon apricot brandy
2 spoons orange juice

Place the ice cubes in the shaker. Pour in the gin, apricot brandy and fresh orange juice, which should first be strained. Stir vigorously for a few seconds and serve in a large cocktail glass or wine glass.

Paradise

42. Parisian

$\frac{2}{5}$ dry gin
$\frac{2}{5}$ dry vermouth
$\frac{1}{5}$ crème de cassis

Prepare in a mixing glass.

4–5 ice cubes
2 spoons dry gin
2 spoons dry vermouth
1 spoon crème de cassis

Place the ice in a mixing glass, which may be chilled. Pour in the gin, the vermouth and the crème de cassis. Stir for a few moments with a long-handled spoon and serve in a large cocktail glass or a wine glass.

Parisian

43. Planters

½ golden rum
½ orange juice
5 dashes lemon juice

Prepare in a shaker with crushed ice.

4–5 ice cubes
4 spoons golden rum
4 spoons orange juice
1 dash lemon juice

Place the ice in the shaker and add the rum and the strained fruit juice (with a spoon of sugar syrup if the oranges are bitter). Stir for a few seconds and serve in a large cocktail glass. This cocktail, which originated in Jamaica, is still very popular today.

Planters

44. Princeton

⅔ dry gin
⅓ port
1 dash orange bitters
1 twist lemon peel

Prepare in a mixing glass.

4–5 ice cubes
2 spoons dry gin
2 spoons port
1 dash natural orange juice
1 twist lemon peel

Place all the ingredients except the lemon peel in the mixing glass. Stir for a few seconds. Pour into a cocktail glass, removing the ice with a strainer, and add the twist of lemon.

Princeton

45. Rob Roy

½ Scotch whisky
½ sweet vermouth
1 dash Angostura bitters

Prepare in a mixing glass with crushed ice.

4–5 ice cubes
3 spoons sweet vermouth
3 spoons Scotch whisky
1 dash Angostura bitters
1 maraschino cherry

Place the ice in a mixing glass, and stir around with a long-handled spoon. Pour away the water and keep back the ice, using a strainer. Pour in the whisky, vermouth and Angostura bitters. Stir for a few seconds. Pour into a cocktail glass and decorate with the cherry.

Rob Roy

46. Rose

$\frac{2}{3}$ dry vermouth
$\frac{1}{3}$ kirsch
1 dash strawberry syrup

Prepare in a mixing glass.

4–5 ice cubes
4 spoons dry vermouth
2 spoons kirsch
1 dash strawberry syrup

Place all the ingredients in the mixing glass. Stir with a long-handled spoon for a few seconds. Serve in a cocktail glass.

Rose

47. Sidecar

½ brandy
¼ Cointreau
¼ lemon juice

Prepare in a shaker with crushed ice.

4–5 ice cubes
2 spoons brandy
2 spoons Cointreau
1 spoon lemon juice

Place the ice cubes in the shaker. Pour in the brandy, the Cointreau and the strained lemon juice. Shake for a few moments and serve in a large cocktail glass or a wine goblet.

Sidecar

48. Stinger

$\frac{2}{3}$ brandy
$\frac{1}{3}$ white crème de menthe

Prepare by stirring together with crushed ice.

4–5 ice cubes
4 spoons brandy
2 spoons white crème de menthe

Place the ice in a shaker, until the shaker is cool. Throw away any water, and pour in the brandy and the crème de menthe. Shake vigorously for a few moments, then serve in a chilled cocktail glass.

Stinger

49. White lady

$\frac{1}{2}$ dry gin
$\frac{1}{4}$ Cointreau
$\frac{1}{4}$ lemon juice

Prepare in a shaker with crushed ice.

4–5 ice cubes
3 spoons dry gin
1 spoon Cointreau
$1\frac{1}{2}$ spoons lemon juice

Place the ice in a shaker. Pour in the gin, the Cointreau and the freshly-squeezed lemon juice, which should be strained. Shake vigorously for a few seconds, then serve in a large cocktail glass or a wine goblet.

White lady

50. Za-za

½ Dubonnet
½ dry gin
1 dash Angostura bitters

Prepare by stirring ingredients together.

4–5 ice cubes
3 spoons Dubonnet
3 spoons dry gin
1 dash Angostura bitters

Place all the ingredients in the shaker. Shake for a few seconds and serve in a cocktail glass, which can be chilled beforehand.

Za-za

The work of a barman

3

The barman

What can the customer expect from a barman? How will he go about his work, and what will be his experience? How and where will he have gained it? It is clear that as in the case of most professions, a barman's work cannot be improvised. Normally, in addition to following a course at a recognized institution, it is necessary to be apprenticed either to a chief barman, or at least to a person of proven experience, and to follow in his footsteps. For, even if it is not possible to follow a formal course of training, (and many barmen who have made a name for themselves are self-taught) it is absolutely indispensable for the student to imitate someone who will be a good example, both so that he understands the work well, and also in order that his career may be rich and satisfying. It follows, then, that the apprentice barman, apart from needing enthusiasm and patience, should try to acquire modesty and a willingness to accept advice (which at the beginning of his apprenticeship may be plentiful) without showing conceit or the mistaken belief that he can get by perfectly well alone. All famous barmen have had good teachers.

To continue our list of the personal qualities which are needed in a barman, in a place open to the public, apart from great forbearance, he will obviously need to keep himself and his surroundings scrupulously clean, and to show unstinting attention and courtesy to his customers. It will be easier to illustrate these with examples, because each detail of correct behaviour has great significance. In fact, forbearance is not only to be seen in the apprentice's attitude towards his teacher (and vice versa) but also in his relations with his customers, who are the real arbiters of his destiny. These customers often make exasperating demands but the barman must show patience, and if possible, even smile.

The apprentice cannot afford to throw his weight around in his dealings with the barman, any more than he can in front of his customers. He must behave as one who is on his way, and not as one who has already arrived. As far as cleanliness and tidiness are concerned there can be no relaxation of the rules: a fresh appearance, an impeccable uniform, and sparkling equipment, neatly set out, count for a lot, as do surroundings which are clean and tidy. These matters, of course, require attention: when the bar itself has been dealt with, the barman has to turn his attention to his equipment and to matters of general organization. Let us consider these aspects of his work one by one.

A fundamental part of organising, for example, is the choice and cataloguing of drinks, and their arrangement in the bar in a particular way so that they are readily to hand, and people can be served as quickly as possible. To this end it is useful to line the bottles up, grouping them according to make or type, or whatever system the barman sees fit. Particular attention must be paid to the glasses which should always be shining and clean.

This brings us to the technical side of preparation, for, as we will see in a later chapter, each cocktail or long drink demands a particular type of glass. It is not initially a good idea when preparing a drink to follow one's own whims: the personal touch can be introduced later. At first it is rather a question of mastering all the basic classic drinks and of having at one's fingertips both the ingredients and the ability to produce an identical drink in any country of the world.

Attention also means psychological observation of the customer. By studying the types of people who make up the clientele, and having a firm theoretical knowledge as a base, the barman will in time be able to anticipate the particular likes and dislikes of his customers – a gift not given to everyone. However, when recommending cocktails and long drinks even the most imaginative suggestions have to follow certain basic rules of how the various drinks may be mixed together. It is clear that certain combinations which cannot be guaranteed to produce favourable results (such as whisky and brandy, grappa and rum, cognac and gin) should be avoided. The fact that drinks rarely asked for are often unpalatable underlines this point. It is, in fact, inadvisable to combine two drinks of high alcoholic content, such as whisky and brandy. It is better to combine a spirit base with other liquids which provide colour and flavour.

From a psychological study of the customer, let us pass on to the final essential attribute which the apprentice barman must have: correctitude, to be understood in both senses of its meaning – respect for others and self-restraint (which are really one and the same thing). There is nothing technical about this quality, it is more a moral, human characteristic. It is not surprising, especially amongst people who always frequent the same bar, that there should, from time to time, be someone who would like to chat with or confide in the barman. The art of listening is not easy, and that of offering sympathy even more difficult. The barman must always remain absolutely silent, listening, but never passing on what he hears. The reason the customer feels he can confide is because he is sure that the barman will not gossip and chat, nor give advice unless asked to. He will avoid criticism and unwanted pleasantries, restricting himself to agreeing with the customer's point of view.

In short, he can never afford to relax his self-control. He must always be prepared for any eventuality. If, for example, as a result of a misunderstanding between the barman and a customer, the customer finds himself with a drink which is not the one he asked for, or the proportions are wrong, it is the duty of the person behind the bar to apologize, and to change the glass politely. (Courtesy almost always works miracles.) This does not, however, mean constant servility and submission; what is needed is tact.

If the fundamental qualities which have been briefly outlined above are not strongly present, then the aspiring barman should attempt to cultivate them if he wishes to succeed in the profession. These qualities are complemented by other, acquired characteristics, derived from practical experience. The first one, of considerable importance in these days of rapid social contact and foreign travel, is some knowledge of at least one (but preferably two), foreign languages. This allows the barman to broaden his professional experience by travel abroad, especially to tourist areas. The second quality concerns the barman's manner, and is acquired by daily contact with people; a willingness which becomes habitual, the calm indulgence of one who knows how to handle people, an unfailing sense of humour, and eventually a philosophical view of life.

Once qualified, then, what sort of position should the barman look for, and where? There is no easy answer, and not even any standard criteria by which to judge the possibilities. Take an enormous city like Tokyo, for example, which has tens of thousands of public bars scattered over the maze of streets which make up one of the most densely populated cities in the world. In each short section of its main streets there are innumerable bars and clubs. In an eight-storeyed building it is possible to find as many as ten: two on the ground floor, two on the first floor, four on the fourth floor, one on the sixth and one on the eighth. And the whole of the city centre is like this.

The bars are in tiny corners, often consisting of only a counter and a tiny store-room, but with two barmen to provide the customer with every variety of drink. When he has finished his drink – thereby automatically becoming a member of the bar-club – the customer goes next door or climbs one flight of stairs to find another. This is how bars are seen in Japan.

When we attempt to enlarge upon the question of where the barman is likely to find himself working, we need to define what 'bar' means in the various countries which have them, and to explain the origin of the name. 'Bar' used to refer to the counter which separated the barman from the customers in the old wineshops. The word now means a place open to the public with no discrimination, where certain rules and conventions are observed. Whether it is simple or grand, it offers a specialised form of service and hospitality. One expects a pleasant place with a counter (housing shelves and bottles, and perhaps a coffee machine) from which customers are served, small tables (these are not essential: it depends upon the size of the establishment and on the style and type of service which the management is aiming to provide), cloakrooms and storage space for the drinks. From this very general description we quickly move on to a consideration of the different types of bars, and for convenience we can divide them into four categories: everyday bars, above-average bars, luxury bars and combination bars.

The simple everyday bar – such as those to be found scattered all over France – merely provides space, service and a range of products sufficient to provide for limited requests from the customers. It is usually an individual, family-run establishment, where the owner and his relations do everything that is necessary for the running of the place. It is not a difficult task to transform such a bar into a more prestigious and lucrative establishment – it merely requires enthusiasm and good sense. Today many of these bars are being brought up to date, and are able to rely upon many modern mechanical aids (from shakers to coffee machines, electrical kitchen gadgets to refrigerated counters) which allow the drinks to be kept in good condition so that the service offered to the customer is improved.

Above–average bars – of which American cocktail bars are typical – offer more spacious and attractive surroundings, with full service and a larger staff. The young barman who, for lack of time or money cannot afford to follow a recognized course, would do best to serve his apprenticeship in one of these bars. Their basic characteristics are not very different from those of the simple bars but, size apart, their style and service is always impeccable. Here, rather than the owner-barman, we often find a barman employed almost exclusively to prepare drinks (cocktails, long drinks, aperitifs, etc) and this lends a certain tone to the establishment.

Then there are the more luxurious bars where refinement, elegance and service reach near-perfection. They are international, often to be found in city centres, near theatres and cinemas, and they seem to be at the same time not too large and impersonal yet able to provide first-rate facilities and service, and to satisfy the requirements of the most demanding customer. They are most often to be found in large hotels, and the barmen who run them have always had an excellent training.

Then – in Germany, for example – one finds the 'combination bars' which belong to large cake shops, and which are noteworthy not only for their sheer size and comfortable surroundings, but also for the unique service they offer.

In Britain, of course, most people expect to visit a pub if they go out to have a drink. While these establishments are historically primarily dedicated to serving beers, nevertheless, many of their landlords and barmen pride themselves on being able to produce a range of mixed drinks and cocktails.

These categories are, obviously, very general ones, but they help to distinguish the different types of work which barmen perform in various countries. It is a world where the barman works at his own pace, in daily contact with a very mixed public, who are sometimes agreeable and sometimes not. Theirs is a world where friendships are made, for at the bar time is often spent in discussing serious problems or current events.

All barmen see what they are doing as an art, a hobby or as work, but not just as one of these three. Only in the rare cases where a person's make-up allows him to fully understand all three does he become the ideal barman. His glance will take in the whole bar as he talks to you, and you will not be sure whether it is a look of satisfaction, or whether he is merely checking that all is well. He will talk to you about his favourite sports, but really all his concentration is engaged in preparing a dry cocktail requested by the usual demanding customer.

The American bar (a barman's paradise) is a machine which functions with a never-ending rhythm, with never a pause from the moment of opening to closing time. It requires constant changes of staff at the bar, and the ability to stay in control however hectic things get. Discipline is the main quality required, although a real professional flair is also needed (for example, in serving the classic international cocktails).

Let us now look at the barman during a delicate moment in his day. In an American bar the hour of aperitifs witnesses a sudden liveliness, as though the lights had just gone up and the curtain had just been raised on the stage. It is the moment which gives the barman his best opportunity for self-expression. All day long he has worked at serving drinks, squeezing fruit, preparing sandwiches and making coffee, but when it is time for aperitifs, he really comes into his own. The colours, the aromas and even the sounds (like the rhythmical noise of the shaker, or the dry thud of the ice as it cracks on contact with the drink in the glass) and the atmosphere of an American bar at aperitif-time all have about them a certain magic. Figures like F. Scott Fitzgerald and Ernest Hemingway may no longer be found there, but from time to time their unforgettable martini cocktails are ordered by someone who remembers those far-off days.

Who, then, are the customers of the modern barman? They include all sorts of people, and cannot be strictly categorized. So, the barman's work, as we have said, is not only to make good cocktails, but above all to establish good relations with the customer, whoever he is, and to make him feel at ease. The cocktail can be identical in two different bars, but the customer will always go back to one of them, because it is there that he finds a certain barman. This is why the aperitif hour, for example, is such an important one. And the barman plays a vital role.

Categories of drinks

After-dinner drinks
Not all drinks classified in this way have to be taken after a meal. A Stinger, for example, which is one of the cocktails recognized by the IBA, is excellent before or after a meal. These after-dinner drinks can

be served cool or ice-cold, or else poured into a good cup of espresso coffee. Who hasn't drunk Irish coffee or grandfather's coffee?

Non-alcoholic drinks
In the United States drinks which belong to this category are known as Shirley Temples. Whether short or long they are made without alcohol. The following ingredients are used: fruit juices such as orange, lemon, pineapple and grapefruit; syrups made from pomegranate, raspberry, black cherry, and strawberry; barley water and citron syrup; mixers such as soda, ginger ale, tonic water, bitter lemon; fresh fruit in season and preserved fruit is used for decoration. These drinks are suitable for any time of day.

Cobblers
These iced and sweetened long drinks are so called because they were invented by a cobbler at the beginning of the eighteenth century. That, at least, was when the drink was first known in England, but in Venice at the time of Marco Polo a drink made from water and wine was already well known. Tastes have changed with the passing of time and from being made with wine and water, then sherry and water, today the Cobbler is made using a wide variety of alcoholic bases. Spirits used must always be of the highest quality. The drink is usually served in a tall glass, decorated with fruit.

Cocktails
A drink containing two ingredients is a mixed drink, while only a drink containing three or more ingredients can be called a cocktail. They are *straight* if undiluted, *on the rocks* if served with ice cubes, and they become *long drinks* when fruit juice or mixers are added. They are often served garnished with slices of orange or lemon.

Collins
The Collins is really part of the family of long drinks. One of the best-known drinks in the world is the Tom Collins, an excellent cocktail, made with gin, lemon juice, sugar syrup, soda water and ice. As well as being an aperitif it is very thirst-quenching, and suitable for all times of day.

Cup
The Cup is an aperitif with a base of sparkling white wine such as champagne or spumante, to which is added a small quantity of spirits and fruit juice. The cup is prepared in a carafe or a bowl, which can be glass or crystal, or even in a large soup tureen. The wine should be ice-cold, and small pieces of apple, pear and peach and slices of orange should be added to it. It should be served in champagne flutes or in chilled glasses, using a ladle.

Daisy
Like all cocktails which use only a little water or soda, the Daisy must be served in a whisky tumbler or Old Fashioned glass. The drink was originally made in the United States, from a spirit plus lime or lemon juice, citron syrup, ice, a little sugar and a little soda.

Eggnog
Eggnog is an excellent combination

Apricot (cup)

On this and the following pages, instructions are given for making cocktails from a range of categories.

for 6–8 people

- *1 apple*
- *4 tinned apricot halves*
- *5 spoons apricot brandy*
- *1 bottle chilled spumante brut*

- *Wash the apple, peel and core it, then cut into circles as shown above.*
- *Put the slices of apple in a large bowl, and place an apricot half on each one. Add the apricot brandy.*
- *Pour in the spumante which has until now been kept in the refrigerator.*
- *Serve in champagne flutes, if possible chilled, using a ladle.*

Doctor (grog)

2 spoons dark rum
2 spoons cognac
1 knob butter
1 teaspoon sugar
1 twist lemon peel
1 clove
juice of $\frac{1}{4}$ lemon
2 spoons boiling water

- *Warm the rum and the cognac in a small saucepan over a very low heat and pour into a punch glass.*
- *Add a knob of butter and the sugar and stir well.*
- *Add the twist of lemon, the clove and the freshly-squeezed lemon juice.*
- *Finally add the boiling water, stir and serve.*

Gold Flip (flip)

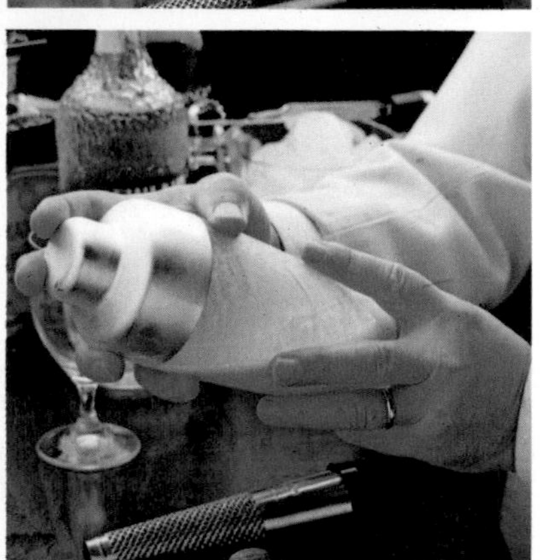

4 ice cubes
2 spoons vodka
2 spoons sweet sherry
2 spoons Amaretto di Saronno
1 egg yolk
2 spoons sugar
nutmeg

- *Place the ice in the shaker and pour in the vodka, sherry and the Amaretto di Saronno.*
- *Add the egg yolk and the sugar.*
- *Shake vigorously for a few seconds.*
- *Pour into a wine glass and grate some nutmeg over the top.*

Haiti (exotic)

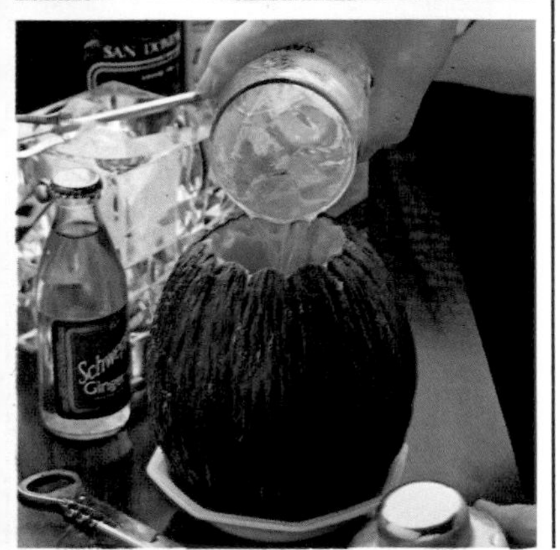

1 melon
4 ice cubes
2 spoons white rum
2 spoons cream sherry
2 spoons Galliano
$\frac{1}{4}$ small bottle ginger ale

- *Using a scoop or a suitable knife, remove the top of the melon and take out the seeds.*
- *Place the ice in the shaker and add the rum, the sherry and the Galliano.*
- *Shake for a few seconds before pouring the mixture and some of the ice into the melon.*
- *Add the ginger ale, stir and serve with straws.*

Irish coffee (after-dinner)

1 *cup hot black coffee*
1 *teaspoon brown sugar*
4 *spoons Irish whiskey*
2 *spoons single cream*

- *Warm the glass with hot water or steam and pour in the coffee.*
- *Add the brown sugar and stir.*
- *Add the whiskey*
- *Finally add the single cream, pouring it over a spoon so that it floats on the surface.*

Italia (pousse café)

3 teaspoons grenadine
1 teaspoon cherry brandy
1 teaspoon white crème de menthe
3 teaspoons anisette
4 teaspoons yellow Chartreuse
a few dashes blue curaçao

- *Pour the grenadine and the cherry brandy into the first small glass; the crème de menthe and the anisette into the second; and the Chartreuse and the blue curaçao into the third.*
- *Stir the red liquid and pour into a tall narrow glass.*
- *Rinse the spoon, stir the white liquid and, using the spoon, pour it a drop at a time on top of the red liquid.*
- *Repeat with the third glass, and you will have all three colours of the Italian flag.*

Sangria

for 6–8 people

1 apple
1 orange
1 clove
10 juniper berries
2 spoons sugar
1 bottle chilled red wine
10 spoons brandy
2 small bottles ice cold soda water

- *Peel and slice the apple and orange and place in a bowl.*
- *Add the clove and the juniper berries.*
- *Add the sugar, a quarter of the wine and the brandy.*
- *Place the bowl in the refrigerator for two hours or in the freezer for twenty minutes, then remove and pour in the remaining wine and soda water. Stir and serve.*

Marie Hélène (crusta)

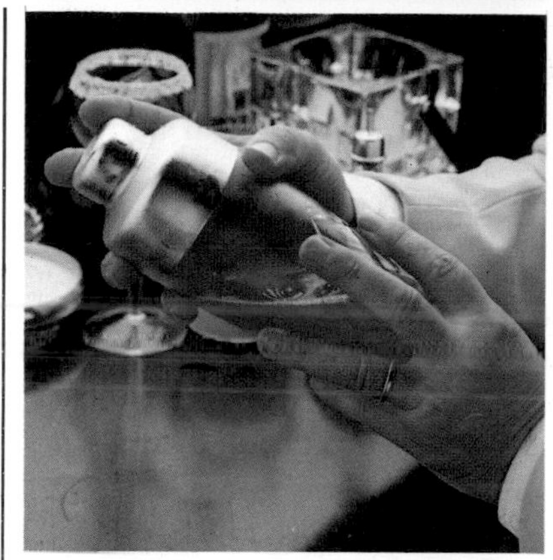

1 lemon wedge
sugar for frosting
4 ice cubes
3 spoons vodka
2 spoons apricot brandy
1 spoon lemon juice
1 spoon orange juice
1 dash grenadine

- *Moisten the rim of the glass with the lemon wedge and immerse in the sugar, then place the glass in the freezer for ten minutes or so.*
- *Place the ice in a shaker. Pour in the vodka, the apricot brandy, the lemon juice and the orange juice.*
- *Add the grenadine.*
- *Shake vigorously for a few seconds and pour the mixture into the glass, taking care to avoid the frosting.*

Oasis (long drink)

4 ice cubes
1 spoon blue curaçao
4 spoons dry gin
½ small bottle soda water
1 slice lemon
1 sprig fresh mint

- *Place the ice cubes in a tall tumbler.*
- *Pour in the curaçao and the gin.*
- *Add the soda water and stir.*
- *Decorate with the slice of lemon and the mint.*

Trinidad (zombie)

4 cubes cracked ice
3 spoons dark rum
3 spoons Aurum
2 spoons apricot juice
1 teaspoon sugar
4 spoons pineapple juice
juice 1 orange
5 spoons white rum
1 slice orange
1 slice lemon
1 slice pineapple
3 maraschino cherries
1 sprig mint

- *Pour into a large glass the dark rum, the Aurum and the apricot juice.*
- *Add the sugar, the pineapple juice, the freshly-squeezed orange juice, and the white rum.*
- *Add the ice and stir.*
- *Decorate with the orange, lemon pineapple, cherries and mint.*

W. Karol (fizz)

4 ice cubes
5 spoons vodka
juice ½ lemon
2 dashes grenadine
½ egg white
1 teaspoon sugar syrup

- *Place the ice in the shaker, which should first have been chilled.*
- *Pour in the vodka, the lemon juice and the grenadine.*
- *Add the egg white and the sugar syrup.*
- *Shake for a few seıonds.*
- *Pour the drink into a tumbler with any remaining ice.*

of milk and egg with the addition of fortified wine or a liqueur. It is prepared in a shaker, with a few ice cubes. Or it can be served hot, as it often is in winter.

Exotic
An Exotic is a cocktail which is made from the pulp of fruit to which liqueurs and the juice of the same fruit are added. It is a good idea to keep the pulp in the freezer until it is to be used.

Fix
A Fix is prepared directly in a medium-sized tumbler, with a liqueur, sugar, water, lemon juice and crushed ice. It is decorated with slices of orange or lemon or with cubes of pineapple or blackcurrants.

Fizz
A Fizz, which is a pleasant drink suitable for any time of day, is made from the white of an egg (or sometimes the yolk), lemon juice, soda water and sugar syrup. One of the most famous is Gin Fizz, which is known throughout the world.

Flip
The Flip originated in the United States. One of the best known is Port Flip, which is made with port, an egg yolk and sugar. Like other drinks, it has changed with time, and is now often made with sherry, marsala and other spirits and liqueurs. It is suitable for all times of day.

Grog
Grog dates from around 1720. It was invented by Admiral Edward Vernon, who is famous for having conquered Panama and Portobello. His crew nick-named him Grog because he wore clothes made out of gros-grain cloth. Returning from a voyage to the Caribbean the Admiral was informed by his first officer that the drinking water had been contaminated, which would normally have meant illness and even death. He ordered that the news be kept quiet, and had the water boiled as quickly as possible. Then he mixed equal quantities of high-quality rum with the water and added sugar to make it more palatable. The mixture was so popular that the crew gave it the same name they used for the Admiral. Later other ingredients came to be added to the drink (such as spices, butter and lemon, and also other spirits such as cognac and whisky).

Julep
The Julep originated in the state of Kentucky in the United States. It is a delicious drink, reminiscent of the country. It is traditionally made with Bourbon whiskey poured on to fresh mint which is first ground with a pestle and mortar. Then crushed ice and sugar are added and the drink is garnished with a sprig of fresh mint. A Julep can also be successfully made using other spirits, such as Scotch, rum, brandy etc.

Long drinks
All mildly alcoholic or non-alcoholic drinks made with fruit juice to which a mixer (soda water, tonic water, ginger ale or bitter lemon) is added belong to this

category. They are prepared directly in a tumbler, some of them having first been shaken. Mixers are added at the last moment, and are never placed in the shaker.

Mist
Although a Mist is one of the easiest drinks to prepare, it usually takes a barman to make it successfully because he has access to an ice-grinder. It is essential that the ice be crushed (even coarsely) if this drink is to be palatable. The tumbler is filled with ice and the liqueur and slice of lemon are then added. This drink is very well known in the United States and is suitable for all times of day.

On the rocks
This is a cocktail which is prepared in a shaker and served in an Old Fashioned glass or whisky tumbler with several ice cubes.

Pick-me-up
This is an alcoholic drink which is also a tonic.

Pousse Café
The Pousse Café consists of a combination of liquids which should not be mixed in the glass. The liqueurs or spirits should be poured slowly, bearing in mind the density of each one, for it is only in this way that a drink in which the different liquids are in separate layers will be obtained. A Pousse Café is served in a special cylindrical glass.

Zombie
The Zombie contains the highest percentage of alcohol of all cocktails. One of the first types of Zombie, a drink which originated in the Caribbean, was prepared in a shaker with crushed ice, lime juice, papaya juice and pineapple juice. The liqueurs used were apricot brandy and light and dark rums. When the drink was ready, about another 5 ml ($\frac{1}{6}$ fl oz) of rum of a lower specific gravity was added to the top.

Equipment

The barman needs many different products and pieces of equipment if he is to please the customer whose appreciation of fine cocktails is always increasing, and whose requests are therefore becoming ever more demanding. New technology, and research and study which has been carried out in this field by companies involved in production have been of great help to barmen, placing at their disposal a whole range of useful and practical equipment which is to be seen in use in almost all the more sophisticated bars.

Tastes have become noticeably more refined as non-professionals have become more closely involved in the fascinating world of cocktails, often wanting to prepare their own at home. Cocktails fall into two main groups – short and long. What we normally refer to as a cocktail is really **a short drink**. These are served in small quantities, usually 100–130 ml ($3\frac{1}{2}$–$4\frac{1}{2}$ fl oz), always well chilled and in a classic wide-topped glass. They tend to be quite strongly alcoholic, since half their volume (the base) consists of a spirit such as brandy, whisky, cognac, gin, vodka or grappa. The other category, **long drinks**, consists of mixed drinks with a preponderance of non-alcoholic ingredients. The addition of fruit juice, syrups and mixers produces a cool, only mildly alcoholic drink. The drink is served in a characteristic tall cylindrical glass, which is known as a tumbler, and which is similar to those normally used for Coca-Cola and other popular drinks.

Whereas a short cocktail is usually served before or after a meal, a long drink is intended above all to be thirst-quenching, and is thus ideal as a summer drink. Its presentation is usually completed by the addition of a slice of orange, lemon, grapefruit, pineapple or other fruit in season for decoration. Many people are under the mistaken impression that the long drink is suitable only for the evening, and requires much preparation. In fact the opposite is true, and not only does it provide an attractive alternative to a fizzy drink, but it is suitable for any occasion. What is more, the proportions are extremely variable, making the drink easy for anyone to make. It is enough merely to follow a few basic rules and to use a little initiative and imagination to obtain acceptable and encouraging results.

The alcoholic content of long drinks is very important and gives the flavour an edge. The aids necessary for making a long drink consist simply of a *tumbler*, a *mixing glass*, a *strainer* and a *long-handled spoon*. The ingredients consist of the usual classic alcoholic substances, which form

the base of the drink, to which a wide variety of other substances can be added, such as fruit juices and mixers. Apart from these, syrups can also be used, making a simple recipe much appreciated when one is feeling hot. Particularly suitable ingredients are citron, mint and raspberry syrups, served with ice or tonic water. It should also be remembered that red and white wine, and also sparkling white wine can be used for simple, original long drinks which are certain to be successful.

More and more people who go out to enjoy cocktails and discover a wide variety of drinks want to analyse how they are made, with a view to stocking their own bars at home. They are then equipped to

Different types of mixing glasses: from the left, a glass one, a crystal one with an ice lip, a glass one with gradations for measuring, a glass one with a lip. In the centre, stirrers in different shapes and different materials.

offer exquisitely-made cocktails and long drinks to guests on special occasions, or simply to enjoy the drinks themselves, sitting in front of the television, comfortably ensconced in an armchair for a short evening of rest after the pressures of the day.

In order that a wide selection of cocktails can be made, it is vital that the bar be stocked with **certain basic products**. Without these it is impossible to work satisfactorily. In a public bar, of course, the range of products is considerably wider, sometimes numbering as many as a hundred varieties. It should be made clear at this point that attempting to have such a wide variety of products available at home is not mere frivolity, but actually necessary for the production of good drinks which are also stylish, exotic, and new or little-known (for the ability to create is one of the main characteristics which separates the real professional barman from a mere mixer of drinks.) The basic products are: a selection of bitters and aperitifs – a bottle each of Campari, brandy, champagne or other sparkling wine, cognac, marsala, port, sherry, vermouths, vodka, gin, rum, grappa, whiskies and a variety of syrups and mixers.

Different types of shakers: from the left, American (part glass part steel); a crystal one (steel top); a plastic one (unbreakable). Centre: a shaker made entirely in steel.

The stock of bottles should also ideally include the following: soft drinks – fresh and canned orange and lemon juice; fizzy drinks – Coca-Cola, beer, soda water, tonic water, mineral water, lemonade, ginger ale; bitters – included in this group are fernet, elixir, china, rhubarb; non-alcoholic syrups – grenadine, citron, peppermint cordial; liqueurs – anisette, framboise, kirsch, tequila, poire william, slivovitz; aperitifs of all sorts – bitter, vermouth, etc; various brandies, cognacs and Armagnacs; sparkling wines – dry, demi-sec and brut, in different-sized bottles; gin – from different countries; grappa – various brands; rum of different colours – Cuban, Jamaican, Mexican; sherry – dry, medium, sweet; vodka – Russian, Polish; whisky – Scotch, Irish, rye, bourbon, Canadian; and a variety of other products – amaretto, apricot brandy, Bénédictine, blue curaçao, green and yellow Chartreuse, cherry brandy, crème de cacao, crème de menthe (green and white), crème de bananes, crème de cassis, orange curaçao, triple sec curaçao and pastis. As well as these it is also important to have fresh and condensed milk, double cream, tomato juice, piquant sauce, fresh eggs and instant coffee.

In addition to the ingredients, certain pieces of equipment are needed for making cocktails. The first is a **mixing glass**, not to be confused with a shaker. This is a large conical glass with a lip, which may be made of glass or crystal and should be used in conjunction with a long-handled spoon whose bowl can also be used as a pestle. The ingredients and the ice are merely stirred together in a mixing glass, whereas in a shaker they are shaken energetically. This is because as well as the alcohol, fruit juices, syrups, eggs, etc. have to be incorporated.

Shakers for shaking cocktails are of various types. The simplest and most widely used is the American (or Boston) shaker, which consists of just two pieces fitted together, while the model usually found in specialist shops is made of three pieces, which has the disadvantage of being difficult to dismantle because sugar tends to get stuck in the joints. Highly decorated shakers are not to be recommended – it is much better to choose a simple one made of glass or metal. Whenever fruit juices are to be used (lemon or orange or grapefruit) it is absolutely essential to buy a stainless steel **strainer**, which should have a surrounding spiral to retain the ice.

A **graduated measuring glass** is also necessary to gauge exactly the quantities of the different ingredients (that is until the level of experience is reached which enables one to gauge quantities with the eye). While on the subject of standardizing measurements, let us establish the liquid volume of the various terms used in the recipes: a dash or small teaspoon – $2\frac{1}{2}$ ml ($\frac{1}{12}$ fl oz); a bar spoon – 5 ml ($\frac{1}{6}$ fl oz); a tablespoon – 10–15 ml ($\frac{1}{3}$–$\frac{1}{2}$ fl oz); a liqueur glass – 30 ml (1 fl oz); a cocktail glass – 115 ml (4 fl oz); a wine glass – 185 ml ($6\frac{1}{2}$ fl oz); a tumbler – 230–285 ml (8–10 fl oz). Fractions refer to the proportion of the contents of a cocktail, regardless of volume.

Continuing the catalogue of equipment necessary to the preparation of cocktails, let us not forget the **ice-bucket**. It can be made of metal, glass or crystal, and usually comes with a pair of tongs for placing ice cubes in the shaker or glass. Also absolutely essential are a **wooden board** for chopping slices of lemon and other fruit, a **small knife** with a wooden handle, a **peel knife** for making twists of peel (equally good results can be achieved with an ordinary knife,

From the left: small glass jug for fruit juice; lemon squeezer; double measure; small measuring jug. From back to front: strainer; nutmeg grater; stainless steel ice spoon with indented bowl; two long-handled forks.

though this takes a little extra patience); a **two-pronged fork** for holding the fruit firm while it is being cut; **cocktail sticks** for cherries, olives, onions or whatever garnish the recipe calls for; paper or cloth **napkins**; a **corkscrew** and a **bottle opener**; paper or plastic **straws** (for long drinks); small **plates** for the 'nibbles' (the savoury snacks which complement the drink); a **soda siphon** (which should

be kept in the refrigerator until needed); and a **carafe** for water.

There are also some electrical gadgets which make the work of the barman or host quicker and easier. First of all there are **orange squeezers**, which may be electrically or manually operated. There is, however, one important drawback to the electric orange squeezer for, although it is easier to use, it also liquidizes the parts of the fruit, such as the skin, which should not

Above: back left, plastic insulated container for ice; right, the same made of steel. Centre. two crystal ice-buckets; a series of ice tongs.

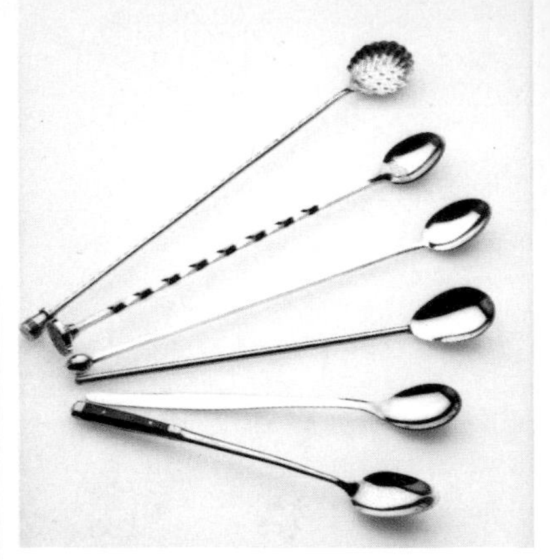

really be used as they make the liquid too thick and heavy. With a manual orange squeezer it is possible to obtain a juice which is clearer and less dense. This result can also be obtained with a centrifuge, a gadget which separates the pulp from the peel using centrifugal force, collecting the clear juice in a special basin. In either case the gadget will certainly be more expensive than a manual orange squeezer.

Another indispensable piece of

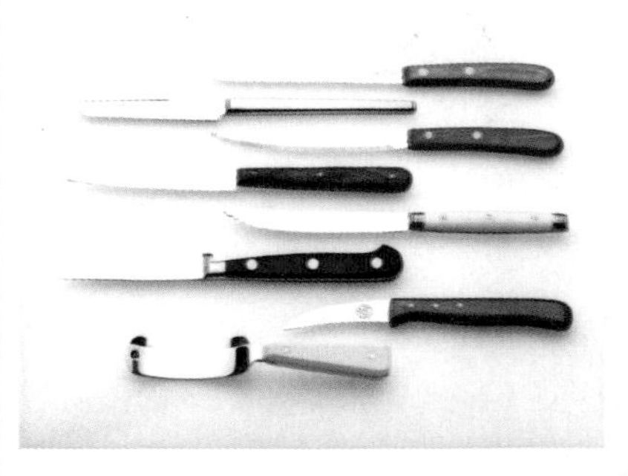

Top: a selection of long-handled spoons (the first for cherries or similar; the others for mixing). Bottom: knives for slicing and peeling fruit.

equipment is an electric **blender**, which is used particularly when the drink has to be whipped (as in frappé, cold zabaglione, and all drinks with an egg or cream base). Then there is the ice crusher, particularly useful for grinding ice finely for use with crème de menthe, anisette, etc.

There is no doubt that of all the ingredients used in mixing drinks ice is the most common of all, for there is hardly a cocktail or a long drink which does not call for it. It is extremely important, however, to remember the rules of hygiene when preparing ice. At home, there is no alternative but to use ice made in the refrigerator or freezer, frozen in special metal or plastic containers, but in a bar the story is different. For in an average bar open to the public, 8–10 kg (18–20 lb) of ice are used every day. If he is to be sure that hygienically-produced ice will always be available, the barman cannot do without an icemaker. Thanks to modern technology, with careful use these machines can last 10–15 years. Apart from being relatively cheap to buy and simple to operate, there is almost no maintenance involved and the machine requires very little storage space. The ice produced by the machine is almost certainly purer and clearer than that obtained by the traditional method (in the freezer), and it also remains frozen longer, and thus does not dilute the alcohol in the drink. Anyone who has to do a lot of home entertaining, and takes the preparation of their cocktails really seriously, might do well to consider acquiring an icemaker.

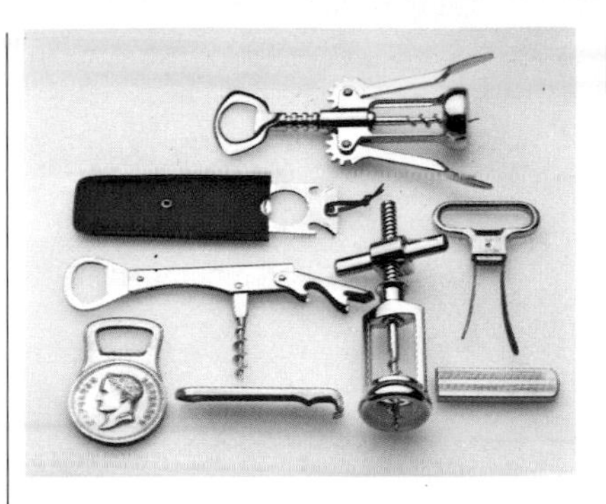

Let us now turn our attention to another very important consideration: the choice of **glass** in which to serve a particular cocktail or long drink. As wide a selection of glasses as possible should be kept, so that each drink can be served in a glass which will allow maximum enjoyment. The glasses are in fact a crucial feature of any bar which prides itself on its reputation: a good cocktail served in the wrong glass will pass completely unnoticed. The use of the correct glass thus becomes the philosophy of the bar. This is governed by a few definite rules but there is also quite a lot of room for originality which should take into account good taste, tradition and the style of the bar.

The range of glasses which every self-respecting bar ought to have is comprised of the following:
cocktail glasses of the classic, wide-rimmed type which are used especially for dry drinks;
whisky glasses (which can also be used for serving long drinks);
balloons – the classic cognac or

Top to bottom, left to right: lever corkscrew, can-opener, waiter's friend, everlasting corkscrew, steel blades (with sheath below), various bottle-openers.

brandy glasses whose characteristic rounded shape brings the drink into contact with the warmth of the hand, so causing the bouquet to be released;
flutes for champagne and sparkling wines – these are tall and elegant in shape and allow the bubbles, which are a natural result of the fermentation of the wine, to rise slowly to the surface of the drink;

Top: wooden cocktail sticks; wide straws; decorative supports for garnishes; little forks for olives, cocktail onions, etc. Above: various soda syphons.

flutes have now largely replaced the traditional classic champagne glass;
sherry glasses, which are squat and rounded and may also be used for port, marsala and sweet vermouth;
tumblers, which are usually used for long drinks – many different shapes and sizes are available, but they consist of two basic types – the tall tumbler and the medium-sized tumbler;
small, slender glasses for sweet liqueurs; they can also be used for vodka and for spirits made from fruit, which should be served well chilled and preferably in a frosted glass;
Old Fashioned glasses, used for all cocktails which require ice cubes, mixers and slices of orange;
rounded, wide-mouthed glasses for soft drinks;
tall, narrow cocktail glasses capable of holding large quantities – particularly suitable for sweet mixtures.

A bar which is equipped with all these glasses is indeed a complete bar. For the bar at home it is of course quite adequate to have just a few types. The ones known as Old Fashioned glasses and tall tumblers are particularly adaptable. They can be used for the many drinks for which a lot of ice or large quantities of liquids are needed, including fizzy drinks. In conclusion, let us remember that although it is true that every type of glass has a specific use, there is also much scope for anyone serving drinks, using their imagination and sense of good taste, to diverge from these rules, which are, in any case, often ill-defined.

Different types of glasses. Top, from the left: open-type champagne glass; small tumbler; Old Fashioned; champagne flute; sherry copita; short drinks glass; tumbler; glass for hot drinks; glass for pousse café. Above, from the left: glass for soft drinks; tall tumbler; balloon; tulip glass; liqueur glass; large capacity glass (for zombies); small goblet; glass for soft drinks; medium-sized tumbler (for drinks on the rocks).

Useful hints

It might, in conclusion, be useful to provide a few tips about the preparation of mixed drinks, and to point out certain basic rules which should be followed at all times.

Ice, which can be taken from the freezer, should be made with fresh water which contains no additives of any kind. If the tap water available contains any sediment or tastes of chlorine, it may be worth using bottled spring water. Ice should not be kept in the refrigerator for long periods, and should always be handled with special tongs, never the fingers.

In order to ensure a plentiful supply of ice at all times, it is a good idea to crush plenty and keep it in the freezer in a container which should first be chilled.

The ingredients used to make cocktails should always be measured out carefully, and it is helpful to use a dessertspoon until one is used to measuring quantities automatically.

The shaker, which is shaken extremely vigorously for just a few seconds, should be used only for mixed drinks when the ingredients include fruit juice, cream, eggs, sweet liqueurs and citrus fruits. It should be cooled before use, and should never be filled more than four-fifths full. The ice should come at least half-way up, whereas in a mixing glass the ice should fill about three-quarters of the glass.

When preparing a cocktail which contains grappa, anisette or crème de menthe, particular care should be taken to ensure that the measurements are accurate, because just a few drops more or less will alter the taste of the drink considerably, as these are highly flavoured substances which will mask the flavours of all the other ingredients. Ingredients should be placed in the shaker or mixing glass in a very definite order: first of all the ice, then the sugar, egg, milk, alcohol and mixers.

To avoid producing large quantities of froth, which is both unnecessary and can spoil the drink, soda, tonic water and sparkling wines are never placed in the shaker or mixing glass, and are instead poured directly into the glass after the part of the drink which has been mixed.

If more than one person is to be served at the same time, whether the cocktail has been mixed in a shaker or in a mixing glass, it should be poured into the glasses in the following way. The glasses should first be lined up side by side. They should all be filled about half-full then the process is repeated until they are all completely full. In this way all the glasses receive an equal share of the ingredients.

Cocktails should be consumed immediately, to avoid changes in smell and taste. There are a few exceptions to this rule: pousse cafè and sangria can be prepared a few hours in advance.

Cocktail glasses should, as a general rule be chilled in advance, so that the drink is kept cool as long as possible. Special glass coolers have been developed for this purpose. If one of these pieces of equipment is not available it will suffice to place the glasses in the freezer, or else to fill them with ice cubes a few seconds before the drink is poured out.

The presentation of cocktails and long drinks is, as we have already noted, also very important, and they should be made to look attractive using decorations such as cherries, slices of orange and lemon or other fruits (all of which should be washed). It is necessary to use great care and a little imagination. One should always use high-quality maraschino cherries rather than those preserved in alcohol or grappa, as these may affect the flavour of the drink.

Prize-winning and imaginative cocktails

4

The first five of the selection of unusual cocktails which follows are ones that are recognized by the International Bartenders Association. As for the fifty international cocktails, the original recipe with proportions of the ingredients is given as well as an adaptation by Gino Marcialis using dessertspoons as a unit of measurement. These are followed by ten cocktails which have won prizes at major national or international events. Where the brand names used by the prize winners are not available, it is possible to substitute other makes of ingredients. Finally, there are fifteen cocktails which have been created especially for this book.

Bellini

IBA recipe for 2 people

$\frac{2}{3}$ *spumante*
$\frac{1}{3}$ *peach juice*

Whip the peach juice with the crushed ice. Pour into a champagne flute, and add the spumante.

---

1 ripe peach
juice $\frac{1}{2}$ lemon
2 teaspoons sugar
$\frac{1}{4}$ bottle iced spumante

Peel the peach and cut into slices, then immerse in the lemon juice (without allowing the flesh to become dark) and place in a blender. Add the sugar and 4 to 5 spoons of spumante. Blend for a few seconds. Pour remaining spumante into chilled champagne flutes, and add the peach mixture.

Harvey wallbanger

IBA recipe

$\frac{1}{3}$	*vodka*
$\frac{2}{3}$	*orange juice*
2	*teaspoons Galliano*

Serve in a tall tumbler or highball glass and add Galliano to the top of the glass without mixing.

4–5	*ice cubes*
4	*spoons vodka*
	juice 1 orange
1	*dash soda water*
1	*spoon Galliano*
1	*slice orange*
1	*slice lemon*
1	*sprig fresh mint*

Place the ice in a tumbler. Pour in the vodka, the strained, freshly-squeezed orange juice and the soda. Stir and add the Galliano on top without stirring again. Decorate with the fruit slices and mint.

Planter's punch

IBA recipe

$\frac{1}{2}$	*golden rum*
$\frac{1}{2}$	*lemon juice*
1	*teaspoon grenadine*
2	*dashes Angostura bitters*
1	*slice lemon*
1	*slice orange*

Mix ingredients together. Pour into a highball glass and add plenty of ice. Decorate with sliced fruit.

4–5	*ice cubes*
5	*spoons white rum*
	juice $\frac{1}{2}$ lime or lemon
2	*spoons grenadine*
2	*dashes curaçao*
	soda water
1	*slice lemon*
1	*slice orange*
1	*maraschino cherry*

Place the ice in the shaker and add the rum, lime or lemon juice and grenadine and shake vigorously. Pour the mixture and ice into a tumbler. Add a little soda water and decorate with the fruit.

Screwdriver

IBA recipe
$\frac{1}{5}$ *vodka*
$\frac{4}{5}$ *orange juice*

Serve with ice in a tumbler.

4–5 ice cubes
5 spoons orange juice
4 spoons vodka
1 spoon sugar or 1 spoon grenadine
1 spoon egg white

Place the ice in a shaker. Pour in the freshly-squeezed, strained orange juice. Add the other ingredients in the order listed above. Shake for a few seconds and serve in a large cocktail glass, or in a tall glass if ice is desired.

Skiwasser

IBA recipe
$\frac{1}{2}$ *lemon juice*
$\frac{1}{2}$ *grenadine*

Place the ice and the other ingredients in a tall glass.

4–5 ice cubes
juice 1 lemon
2 spoons raspberry syrup
$\frac{1}{2}$ *small bottle soda water*
1 maraschino cherry

This long drink should be prepared directly in the tumbler. Pour in all the ingredients listed above, then stir with a long-handled spoon and decorate with the cherry.

AMBA

by G. R. Echenique
(Argentina)

International Cocktail
Competition 1965
(Buenos Aires)

$\frac{4}{10}$	*Old Smuggler Scotch whisky*
$\frac{3}{10}$	*Estelar Pampero golden rum*
$\frac{2}{10}$	*Cinzano rosso vermouth*
$\frac{1}{10}$	*apricot brandy*
	lemon juice
1	*maraschino cherry*

Prepare in a mixing glass. May be served with a few ice cubes. Decorate with the maraschino cherry.

Carin

by George de Kuypers (Belgium)

International Cocktail Competition 1958 (Brussels)

$\frac{1}{2}$ *Gordon's dry gin*
$\frac{1}{4}$ *Dubonnet*
$\frac{1}{4}$ *Isolabella mandarin liqueur*
juice 1 lemon

Prepare in the shaker with a few ice cubes. Can also be served *on the rocks* (with a few ice cubes in a medium-sized tumbler).

Champion

by Hans Durr
(Switzerland)

International Cocktail Competition 1962 (Hamburg)

- $\frac{3}{10}$ *Cinzano dry vermouth*
- $\frac{3}{10}$ *White Label Scotch whisky*
- $\frac{2}{10}$ *Bénédictine*
- $\frac{2}{10}$ *Bols white curaçao*

Prepare in the shaker with a few ice cubes. May also be served *on the rocks* (in a medium-sized tumbler with a few ice cubes).

Long sprint

by Alberto Bramucci (Italy)

Italian National Cocktail Competition 1973 (Venice)

$\frac{1}{4}$	*Royal Stock brandy*
$\frac{1}{4}$	*Martini dry vermouth*
$\frac{1}{4}$	*Galliano*
$\frac{1}{4}$	*Isolabella mandarin liqueur*
	George Goulet champagne
	candied fruit

Prepare in a mixing glass with ice. Pour the ingredients into a tall glass and fill up with champagne, decorating with candied fruit (citron and cherries).

Luisita

by Amato Dido (Italy)

Italian National Cocktail Competition 1966 (St Vincent)

$\frac{3}{4}$	*Bols blue curaçao*
$\frac{1}{4}$	*barley water*
	a few dashes lemon juice
	soda water

Prepare directly in the glass, adding soda water to taste.

Raffino

by Raffaele Floridia (Italy)

Italian National Cocktail Competition 1965 (St Vincent)

2/5	*Martini bianco vermouth*
1/5	*Bosford gin*
1/5	*Campari*
1/5	*Duval cordial*
1	*slice orange*
2	*cherries*

Prepare in the glass with a few ice cubes. Decorate with orange and cherries.

Ramcooler

by Fred Falkemberg
(Canada)

International Cocktail
Competition 1976
(St Vincent)

$1\frac{1}{4}$ oz (35.4 ml) Bacardi white rum
$\frac{1}{2}$oz (15 ml) Galliano
2 oz (57 ml) lime juice
1 slice lime
1 cherry

Prepare in the shaker with crushed ice. Pour the mixture into the glass with the ice. Decorate with the cherry.

Sanremo 72

by Tonino Palazzi
(Italy)

European Festival of Cocktails 1972
(San Remo)

½	*grapefruit juice*
¼	*Bols triple sec*
¼	*Isolabella mandarin liqueur*
	Laurent Perrier brut champagne
1	*slice grapefruit*
1	*slice mandarin*
1	*radish*

Prepare directly in a large glass, topping up with champagne, and decorating with grapefruit, mandarin and radish.

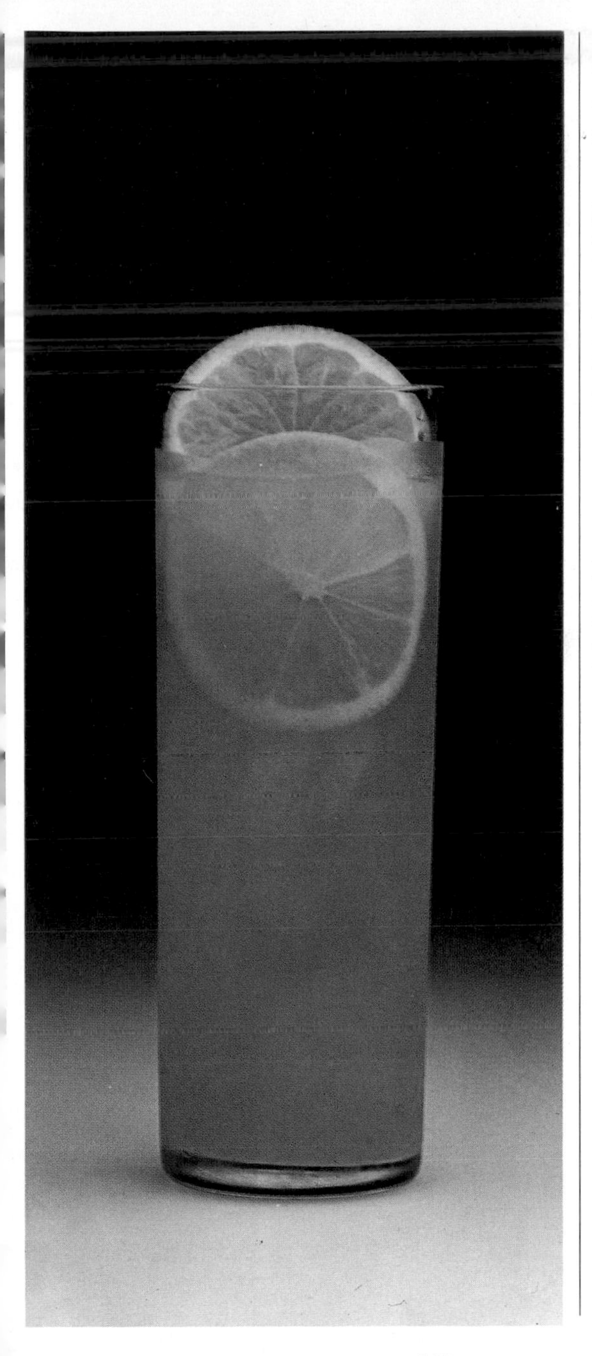

Sbarbina

by Mario Maruccetti (Italy)

Italian National Cocktail Competition 1970 (St Vincent)

$\frac{2}{5}$	*Bosford gin*
$\frac{3}{20}$	*Sis apricot brandy*
$\frac{2}{5}$	*orange juice*
$\frac{1}{20}$	*Isolabella grenadine*
	Cinzano dry spumante
1	*slice orange*
1	*slice lemon*

Prepare directly in a glass with a few ice cubes, and top up with spumante. Decorate with orange and lemon.

Tuttosì

by Elio Cattaneo
(Italy)
International Cocktail
Competition 1969
(St Vincent)

$\frac{4}{10}$ *Canadian Club whiskey*
$\frac{2}{10}$ *Royal Stock brandy*
$\frac{2}{10}$ *Martini red vermouth*
$\frac{1}{10}$ *Galliano*
$\frac{1}{10}$ *Isolabella mandarin liqueur*
juice of 1 orange

Prepare in a mixing glass. May also be served *on the rocks* in a medium-sized tumbler with a few ice cubes.

Adam

3–4 ice cubes
3 spoons calvados
1 spoon Galliano
1 spoon mandarin liqueur
4 spoons pineapple juice
4 spoons orange juice
juice ½ grapefruit
1 slice pineapple
2 small scoops apple
1 maraschino cherry

Pour the ingredients into a large glass. Stir together and decorate with the pineapple, the apple scoops (made with a melon-baller) and the maraschino cherry.

Barcarola

4–5 ice cubes
3 spoons Pernod
2 spoons Sacco Verde crème de menthe
1 strip cucumber peel
1 sprig fresh mint
iced water

Place the ingredients into a tumbler. Add water to taste and stir with a long-handled spoon. Decorate with the cucumber and the sprig of mint.

Bruna

3 *spoons Jack Daniel's whiskey*
2 *spoons Cinzano rosé vermouth*
1 *spoon Bols crème de bananes*
4–5 *ice cubes*
½ *bottle ginger ale*
¾ *banana*
1 *maraschino cherry*
1 *sprig mint*

Pour the first three ingredients into a large glass, and add the ice and the ginger ale. Stir with a long-handled spoon. Decorate with the banana, the cherry and the mint. Serve with a straw.

Cadoni cooler

4–5 *ice cubes*
3 *spoons Tullamore Dew Irish whiskey*
3 *spoons green curaçao*
½ *small bottle ginger ale*
fruit in season

Place the ice in a tumbler and add the whiskey, the curaçao and the ginger ale. Stir and add the fruit, cut into small pieces. Stir again and serve with straws.

Grandfather's coffee

2 spoons brandy
1 spoon Amaretto di Saronno
1 cup sugared espresso coffee

Warm the brandy and liqueur in a small saucepan over a low heat for a few seconds; then pour them into a warm brandy balloon and add the hot coffee.

Campari and orange

4–5 ice cubes
juice 1 orange
4 spoons Campari
1 teaspoon strawberry syrup
1 dash soda water
1 slice orange

Place the ice in the shaker, then pour in the strained orange juice, the Campari and the strawberry syrup. Shake vigorously for a few seconds. Pour the mixture and any ice which remains in the shaker into a tumbler. Add the dash of soda and decorate with the slice of orange.

Cordial cobbler

3	*spoons Campari cordial (premixed, non-alcoholic Campari)*
2	*spoons Perla dry maraschino*
2	*spoons crushed ice*
3	*spoons soda water*
1 or 2	*maraschino cherries*
	fruit in season

Place the ingredients in a wine goblet in the order shown above. Stir and decorate with the fruit, cut into small pieces.

Daisy

2	*spoons roughly crushed ice*
4	*spoons white rum*
1	*spoon Amaretto di Saronno*
1	*teaspoon barley water*
1	*teaspoon grenadine*
¼	*small bottle tonic water*
1	*slice kiwi (or other exotic fruit)*
1	*maraschino cherry*
1	*medium-sized daisy or marguerite*

Place the ice in an Old Fashioned glass or a tumbler. Pour in all the liquid ingredients and stir gently. Decorate with the slice of exotic fruit, the cherry and the flower (wrapping the stem with a piece of foil).

Strawberry brut

3	*strawberries*
1	*teaspoon maraschino*
	iced dry spumante

Place the strawberries in a chilled champagne flute. Pour in the maraschino and fill up the glass with the spumante.

Gold velvet

1	*spoon natural pineapple juice*
½	*bottle iced beer*
½	*chilled champagne*

Pour the freshly-squeezed pineapple juice into a large glass or tumbler. Add the beer and stir. Finally pour in the champagne, slowly, and without stirring again.

Hawaiian doll

4–5 ice cubes
2 spoons white rum
2 spoons Martell cognac
2 spoons Galliano
2 dashes grenadine
2 dashes natural pineapple juice
juice of ½ grapefruit
1 slice orange
2 maraschino cherries

Place the ice and all the liquid ingredients in a tumbler or large glass and stir with a long-handled spoon. Decorate with the orange and cherries.

Old William

4–5 ice cubes
4 spoons Pera Segnana pear liqueur
1 spoon Perla dry maraschino
1 spoon orange juice
1 spoon lemon juice
1 slice lemon
1 slice orange

Place the ice cubes in the glass. Pour in the pear liqueur, the dry maraschino and the fruit juices. Stir with a suitable spoon and decorate with the orange and lemon.

Midnight sun

4–5 ice cubes
3 spoons Finlandia vodka
3 spoons apricot brandy
$\frac{1}{4}$ egg white
2 apricot halves
juice 1 lemon

Place all the ingredients in the shaker except the apricot halves (which can be tinned). Shake for a few seconds and pour into a medium-sized tumbler. Decorate with the apricot halves.

Tour d'argent

1 teaspoon Martell cognac
1 teaspoon Cointreau
1 large champagne flute or wine goblet of well-chilled champagne
1 sugar cube
1 dash blue curaçao
1 slice orange

Place the cognac and the Cointreau in the glass, and fill up with champagne. Place the slice of orange on the surface. Sprinkle the sugar cube with curaçao and rest on top of the slice of orange.

The components of cocktails

5

Alcohol
When we talk about alcohol, we are usually referring to the ethylic variety which is present in the various alcoholic drinks which people have been producing since time immemorial. Alcoholic drinks can be divided into three distinct groups according to the way in which they are made. There are those made by fermenting must, which is unfermented juice or pulp – such as wine and beer. Then there are those made by distilling the fermented must – such as brandy. And finally there are those which contain alcohol in various amounts, and which are flavoured with different extracts and essences and sweetened with sugar or other sweet substances – such as anisette.
The percentage of alcohol present varies from about 3% in the lightest of beers, to a maximum of 60–80% in certain spirits (such as grappa, rum and vodka). Apart from ethyl alcohol, all drinks contain other substances which determine their particular characteristics – taste, smell, bouquet, attractiveness and quality. These other substances, which are present in very small quantities, are: methyl alcohol, propyl alcohol, isobutyl alcohol and other superior kinds of alcohol. Also present in alcoholic drinks to a greater or lesser degree, depending on the method by which the drink is produced, are tannic acids and substances which give smell to the drink as well as salt and sugar.
In any case, every alcoholic drink, whatever its components, has a certain dietary value, which is provided by the alcohol itself. At this point we ought to stop and consider the question of whether alcohol can really be called food. If we think of it as a source of calories, the answer is undoubtedly positive. It is rapidly absorbed by the stomach, and only a small quantity is expelled (via the lungs and the kidneys) while the rest is metabolized to produce energy. This metabolic process takes a fair amount of time (about 10–15 ml or ½ fl oz of alcohol is metabolized in an hour) and it is for this reason that the unpleasant effects of too much alcohol take so long to wear off.
But the harmful effects of excessive amounts aside, it is a fact that alcohol in one form or another represents a habitual element in the diet of most people, and for this reason its dietary importance as well as its social significance ought to be taken into consideration. One estimate has calculated that the average worker consumes approximately 115 ml (4 fl oz) of alcohol per day, which represents 800 calories, or 30% of his calorific intake. Any alcohol taken over and above this amount is excessive (both to his dietary needs and his alcoholic tolerance).
The ethane present in alcoholic drinks can also set in motion certain pharmacological processes. Taken in small quantities, alcohol has a direct effect on the mucus of the stomach, encouraging the secretion of gastric juices without altering the motility of the organ. It also has a vasodilatory effect on the arteries and the coronary arteries, which causes the blood to flow faster without overworking the cardiac muscles. Many studies in recent years have pointed out the relief from pain to be gained by sufferers from the heart disease angina pectoris by taking a small quantity of a very strongly alcoholic drink (such as cognac, whisky or rum). Alcohol has also been shown to be of use in cases of kidney disease. As for its effect on the nervous system, alcohol is naturally a depressant and not a stimulant so, taken in small quantities after an evening meal, it produces a pleasant sensation of relaxation and well-being.

Amaretto di Saronno
This dessert liqueur is made from almonds and has a delicate, intense and velvety taste. It is often drunk neat, though its delicate taste and strong, intense aroma make it particularly suitable for inclusion in cocktails, frappés and ice-cream cups, fresh fruit salads and other desserts. The story of Amaretto di Saronno goes back to the 16th century when a famous painter from Lombardy, Bernardino Luini, received from an innkeeper whose portrait he had painted a delicately-flavoured amber-coloured drink which had been made by leaving apricot kernels to soak in brandy.

Amer Picon
This liqueur is popular as an aperitif and an after-dinner drink. It is made from gentian, orange and cinchona bark, according to an original recipe invented by Gaetano Picon in 1837 and has remained unchanged since. Served with soda-water it makes an excellent long drink which is thirst-quenching and acts as a tonic.

Angostura bitters
The main component of Angostura bitters, which is a fundamental ingredient of many cocktails, is the bark of the cusparia tree (*Cuspari officinalis*), which belongs to the Rutacea family. The oil extracted from the bark is bitter and astringent. Other tropical trees in the Rutacea family

may also be used: *Cusparia felcifuga*, and *Esemleckia felcifuga*.
The recipe for Angostura bitters was invented in 1824 by Johan Gottlieb Siegert, a young German doctor who, after fighting in the Prussian army against Napoleon, developed a love of adventure and freedom, and went to South America to offer his services to the Venezuelan army (under General Simon Bolivar) which was engaged in a struggle to avoid Spanish domination. The young Siegert soon realized that one of the most urgent problems to be dealt with was that of finding a remedy for the stomach complaints from which the soldiers were suffering. He studied the herbs and spices of the country for four years, measuring them and distilling them carefully, until at last he hit upon the ideal formula. He named his preparation Angostura, after the city where he had worked and which is now known as Ciudad Bolivar.
Angostura soon became known all over the world, even though its use differs from that for which it was originally formulated. As well as being widely used in cocktails, it is very useful in cooking, by virtue of its taste and its delicate perfume.

Anisette
This liqueur, with its clear, crystalline colour and refreshing flavour was first made by the inhabitants of ancient Egypt, Babylon and Greece by combining a distillate of anise with several aromatic herbs. It has medicinal values and is particularly suitable as an after-dinner drink, as it aids digestion.

Apricot brandy
This is made using a distillate of carefully-selected apricot juice which is then mixed with sugar. It is usually left to mature in oak casks. When fruit flavouring is used instead of fresh apricots, the resulting liquid cannot be called apricot brandy, but is known as apricot liqueur. These are both useful in the preparation of cocktails and long drinks.

Armagnac
The oldest of French grape brandies, famous and much praised for its subtle, gentle bouquet, armagnac has been distilled in Gascony for over 500 years. The wine must be made by traditional methods with no additions; distillation is carried out in a single step in copper stills, and the brandy that is drawn off is aged in casks, handmade from Monlezun forest oak. When fully matured, armagnac is transferred to older casks; then blending starts. No armagnac may be less than three years old, though many are considerably older. The white wine used must come from specified vines from a limited area which is divided into three regions: Haut (or white) Armagnac, Tenareze, and Bas (or black) Armagnac whose very delicate prune-flavoured brandies are considered the best. As well as being savoured in a brandy balloon, armagnac is used in long drinks and cocktails.

Aurum
This drink is made by mixing a distillate made from vintage Italian wines with one made from oranges. Vintage wines give a distillate which, when matured in small oak casks, takes on the characteristic colour of the wood. It is left to mature in cellars for at least four years to produce a high-quality brandy. Meanwhile oranges and other carefully-selected citrus fruits are first infused, using a very old recipe, and then mixed with other flavourings and fine brandies. This infusion is then distilled three times, until the product assumes the desired flavour and alcoholic strength. The two distillates are finally mixed together and left to mature in the cellars of the distillery. The success and popularity of Aurum brandy is partly due to Gabriele d'Annunzio who, although he was a teetotaller, praised its quality in some of his writings, and gave it the name by which it is known today.

Bacardi
This fine white rum originated in Cuba but is now produced in Puerto Rico and Nassau. In Europe, because of its lightness, it has achieved great popularity as a base for cocktails.

Barolo
Barolo liqueur, used in cocktails, is flavoured with cinchona bark and its base is Barolo wine which is dark in colour, has a strong bouquet and a velvety full-bodied taste. The pride of the Italian wine industry, Barolo is produced from the *Nebbiolo* vine, grown in a particular part of the province of Cuneo. To merit the name Barolo it has to be matured for at least four years (excluding the year of harvest), and three of these must be in oak or chestnut casks, but the wine reaches perfection after eight years.

Beer
The origins of beer go back 8,000 years. One of the oldest examples of proto-cuneiform writing, found on the banks of the river Euphrates, now known as the *Blau Monument* and kept in the British Museum, makes a clear reference to beer. Nebuchadnezzar, the famous king of Babylon, also thought highly of it,

and as well as drinking it the people used it during sacrificial ceremonies to please the gods. Other references to the drink can be found in ancient Egypt, where, for example, mugs full of beer were found next to the pharaoh's mummy in the Sakkara pyramid.

Brewing methods were improved, and from Egypt the drink soon spread throughout the known world. It reached Greece, where it became so popular that Hippocrates, the famous doctor, said of it that it 'quenches the thirst, does not swell the stomach, and causes no problems to the digestion'. Beer soon became the national drink amongst the Celtic peoples, and was considered a gift from the goddess of agriculture. Around 1258 King John of Brabant, better known as King Gambrinus, earned himself the nickname of the beer king, because he refused to drink anything else.

Some 500 years ago hops began to be added to beer, and became universally used in Britain about 250 years ago. As the importance of hygiene in preparing beer was not understood, the liquid often became contaminated and sour. Hops were among the strongly flavoured plant substances used to disguise this. Then it was found that beer with hops kept better. The reason, not understood at the time, was that, as well as adding an interesting flavour, the bitter substances limited the growth of infective agents. In the middle of the last century Louis Pasteur first showed how food and drink can be spoiled by microbacterial activity. The brewing industry applied this knowledge and began the strict control of production and quality that exists today.

All beer is the product of fermentation by yeast of carbohydrates in cereals. The cereals used in different parts of the world include maize, rice, millet, oats, rye, wheat and barley. In Britain malted barley is used, together with small quantities of adjuncts such as unmalted barley, wheat, rice and maize. First the malting barley is encouraged to germinate, then, some five days later, the growth is stopped by drying and heating the grain. This process, which also darkens the colour, can be controlled to produce the malt basis for different types of beer. The malt is then crushed to grist and 'mashed' with pure water at the correct temperature. Various crushed, unmalted cereals can be added at this stage, too, while sugar adjuncts may be added after the liquid wort has been separated from the spent grains. The sweet wort is then boiled with hops, after which the strained, hopped wort is fermented with carefully selected yeasts. About five days later the beer is run off into storage containers. It can then be matured and go through the various final stages which enable it to 'come into condition' and be ready to drink.

According to recent authoritative studies made at various European universities, beer aids digestion and stimulates the secretion of gastric juices. It is recommended in many cases: for old people, whose bodily functions have slowed down; for sick people, to speed their recovery; during pregnancy, because beer contains many easily-assimilated phosphates and vitamins; for nursing mothers, because it stimulates a larger production of milk; for sportsmen and women because it is energy-producing and has a high vitamin content. It provides approximately three-quarters the amount of energy as the same volume of milk. Furthermore, analysis has shown that it has the lowest alcohol content of all popular drinks, but the highest content of nutritious substances (malt, sugar, amino acids, vitamins, mineral salts).

Unlike wine, beer cannot be stored for a long time, and above all should not be exposed to the sun. After purchase, the best way of storing it is undoubtedly in the refrigerator, and the bottles should be placed in such a way that they can easily be removed in order of the date of purchase. The temperature at which beer should ideally be served is around 7–8°C (45°F). If it is too cool, the full flavour cannot be enjoyed, and the thick froth, which is very important at least to the appearance of the drink, cannot be obtained.

Bénédictine

The origins of Bénédictine go back a very long time. The liqueur is prepared by mixing together and distilling various herbs and flavourings according to a recipe which was originally created by the Benedictine monks of the Norman city of Fécamp in 1610, and jealously guarded by them ever since. The bright yellow colour of the liqueur and its strong alcoholic content are the result of a very long ageing process. It is very good drunk straight or used in mixed drinks.

Bitters

These are alcoholic tinctures of bitter roots and barks, flavoured in various ways and possessing a tonic action on the digestive system. Among the aromatic herbs and spices generally used are cardamom, vanilla, cinnamon, cloves and coriander. The bitter flavour may be imparted from plants such as aloes, wormwood, cinchona,

chinese rhubarb, and gentian.
First the different plants have to be gathered, then they are inspected and finally undergo one of two processes: infusion and distillation. The greenery and roots which contain a high level of oils and important essences are passed straight for infusion. They are pulverized and immersed in an oak butt containing hydro-alcoholic solution, in which they are left to soak for many months. When this period has elapsed the liquid is made as clear as possible, ready to join the distilled liquid.
Plants and roots which are not so succulent are given a different treatment. They are immersed in an alcoholic solution without being pulverized, and this is then brought to the boil. The alcohol evaporates and is collected in refrigerated channels, where it condenses and passes in liquid form into special tanks. Distilled liquid obtained in this way also has to undergo a maturation before it is mixed with the liquid obtained by infusion in special steel containers.
The two components are mixed together mechanically, and alcohol and sugar syrup are added. When this process is over, the product is left to age naturally in enormous oak casks, where it matures, and its characteristic taste and smell are released.
Bitters may, roughly speaking, be divided into three categories: sweet, dry and bitter. The ones which belong to the first group are those with a distinct *sweet* taste which are usually pale in colour. *Dry* bitters, on the other hand, are characterized by a bitter taste and are dark brown in colour. Those which have a decidedly *bitter* taste are jet-black in colour.
Here is a description of the composition of a few typical bitters. *Fernet*, for example, is made up of laurel leaves, aloes, anise, wormwood, cardamom, cinnamon, cascara, coriander, liquorice and nutmeg. For *centerbe* the following are among those used: achillea, milfoil, anise, orange, basil, cinnamon, camomile, lemon-scented verbena, clover, juniper, mint, nutmeg, rosemary, sage, teas and vanilla. *Elixir di Quinquina* contains: cinchona, orange peel, cinnamon, *eugenia caryophillata* and *illicium verum* (a form of anise).
Monasteries and convents all over the world have a long tradition of preparing infusions and liqueurs, including bitters. The walnut liqueur, for example, made by the Trappists of Guardistallo and the *erbamaro* of Mount Olivetti are based on age-old recipes which have been kept secret for one generation after another. The main ingredient of the *walnut liqueur* is unripe nuts, whose husks are rich in tannic acids. About fifteen are needed for every litre of liqueur, and they are gathered, so the story goes, on Saint John's day (24 June). Often cloves, cinnamon, lemon peel, a pinch of thyme, sweet wine and grappa are also used, especially if a more robust product is desired. It takes at least two years to produce a good walnut bitter.
Erbamaro is prepared by making an infusion of twenty-two herbs, which are gathered near Mount Olivetti. Those used are angelica, melissa, thyme, eucalyptus, wormwood, hyssop, sage and many others. It takes about twelve months to prepare. The exact origins of the recipe for this bitter are unknown, but it probably first came from France, imported by a Benedictine monk at the end of the last century.
Bitters are normally taken as after-dinner drinks, but they are also popular as aperitifs, served with mineral or tonic water in a tall glass with ice and a slice of lemon. Bitters are used in the preparation of many excellent cocktails.

Bourbon

Bourbon whiskey gets its name from Bourbon county (named after the Bourbons who were on the throne of France at the time). This is a particularly fertile area in the interior of the American state of Kentucky which has a moderate climate. The first Kentucky whiskey was distilled in Bourbon county from maize ground at the mill of a Baptist pastor, Elijah Craig, in the autumn of 1789. Soon excellent whiskey became renowned throughout the county and by 1810 there were 2,000 distilleries producing it. Barrels of it were transported to the mountain regions and valleys of the Ohio and Mississippi rivers. Shopkeepers and hunters introduced it to the American Indians and pioneers carried it across the plains to the far-off West. In this way the fame of Bourbon whiskey spread.
It is produced from high-quality cereals such as maize, rye, and barley, which are chosen by experts, but the mash used must by law not be less than 51% maize. The maize and rye are cut up, boiled and mashed together, then the barley is added. The result is a malt mixture to which pure yeast is added to cause fermentation and the production of alcohol. The fermented mixture is then boiled in a still to release the alcohol. The alcohol, which becomes vapourized, is then cooled and distilled

again, increasing the alcoholic concentration. The bourbon is then laid down for a period of four to six years, during which time the alcohol matures slowly in light oak casks. These are stored in special cellars where temperature and humidity are checked constantly. The product is not bottled until it has matured sufficiently. Although the techniques of distillation have, without a doubt, been modernized since the days of rudimentary stills, the art of producing excellent Kentucky bourbon has, nevertheless, remained virtually the same through the years.

Calvados
This is the apple brandy produced under rigorous control specifically in the Calvados district of France. There are various *appellations* whose quality and character are determined by the soil where the apples are grown, the manner in which the cider is distilled, the period of ageing in oak casks and the blending. Calvados must be aged for two years, and about 70% is drunk young while the remainder is drunk after ageing for six years. There are many ways of drinking it – added to coffee, mixed with fruit juices as a long drink, as the basis of cocktails, sipped neat after dinner, or, to aid the digestion, knocked back in a single gulp between courses of a meal.

Campari
A pleasant bitter aperitif, made from a hydroalcoholic infusion of aromatic plants, fruit and herbs, using an old classic recipe which belongs to the famous Milanese company which produces the drink. Campari is a drink which is known all over the world, and, because of its taste and characteristic bright red colour, forms an essential element in the recipes for many cocktails and long drinks.

Campari cordial
A liqueur which is made by allowing raspberries to soak in brandy, distilling the liquid, then maturing it for a long time in oak casks. The final product which results from the special and secret processes carried out by the Milanese producers, is clear, sweet and strongly alcoholic. A non-alcoholic cordial is also manufactured, but neither is widely available outside Italy. Campari cordial makes an excellent after-dinner drink and has also recently come to be served with ice, as well as being a fairly common ingredient of cocktails, especially those with a particularly delicate flavour.

Canadian whiskey
This spirit is made from rye, barley malt and small quantities of wheat and other grains, and, as with all whiskies, the water used contributes to the characteristic flavour and aroma. The slow maturation process has a critical effect, too, as it takes place in charred white oak casks, and blending is done with many component whiskies. Canadian whiskey is a very smooth drink in its own right, and in the preparation of cocktails has the advantage of not imparting too strong a flavour.

Champagne
For a long time champagne, which is the product of one of the lesser wine-growing areas of France, was merely an excellent red wine with a slight tendency to be fizzy and blow the corks out of the bottles, much to the despair of the producers. Vineyards were already being cultivated in this area in the first centuries AD, and they were rapidly developed in the middle ages. Champagne was perfected by a Benedictine monk, Dom Perignon, steward of the Abbey of Hautvilliers from 1668 to 1715. He was a chemist and physicist as well as a connoisseur of wine, and he began to experiment along three different lines. He experimented with different blends – even breaking the rules of wine-making which had until then been applied, but thanks to his very sensitive palate he was able to tell in advance what the result of any combination would be. He also tried using corks instead of the layer of oil, which had been used up till then, and he discovered what circumstances encourage fermentation in the bottle, causing fizziness. He observed that this particular wine 'hibernated' during the winter and 'woke up' in the spring. He then had the idea of using this period of rest to stopper the wine firmly in the bottle, thus conserving the gas formed during the spring fermentation. This gas produces the *mousse* (bubbly froth), which becomes finer the more slowly the fermentation takes place. Dom Perignon's discoveries gradually became widely known; at the same time cork stoppers were invented, as well as bottles which were perfectly smooth on the inside and strong enough to withstand great pressure from the gases in the wine. Around the middle of the 19th century the use of red wine gave way to white wine, and champagne as we know it today began to be produced. Pasteur, who confirmed and applied the discoveries of the preceding years in a scientific way, made his contribution to champagne production, too.
Champagne may only be produced on land specified in the decree of 17

December 1908 – in the *départements* of Marne and Aisne (whose boundaries are very clearly specified), which are to be found to the east of Paris, near the cities of Reims and Epernay. In this area the soil is mostly limestone, which is rich in fossils and well-suited to growing chardonnay vines (which have green grapes), and pinot noir and pinot meunier (which have black grapes), the only varieties from which champagne can be produced. According to the proportions he uses of wine made from green grapes and white wine made from black grapes, each producer obtains his own particular champagne, which must be produced according to strict laws that enforce the ban in the province of Champagne on the production of natural sparkling wines made in large containers, and ensure that the wine really is what its label claims.

The harvest and preparation, which takes place towards the end of September, follows a rigorous pattern during which the pips are discarded. Every year a law sets the quantity of grapes which can be picked from each hectare of land, and any grapes over and above this amount may not be used (this, of course, helps to ensure that those picked are of a high quality). The grapes from different vines are pressed immediately, and the fresh juice is taken to the cellars, where the wine-making process begins.

The method used for making champagne involves a whole series of delicate and complex operations, from fermentation to ageing. Normal fermentation is followed by the usual procedures which are carried out when white wine is made, and then the *cuvée* (blending) is performed, when wines from different *crus* (small areas characterised by particularly favourable weather, soil and aspect) and from the different types of vine grown in the champagne area, are mixed. The next stage is bottling: a small amount of *liqueur de tirage* (sugar dissolved in matured champagne) is added to encourage the second fermentation and the production of carbon dioxide (the *prise de mousse* or carbonage) in the hermetically-sealed bottle.

There then follows the *remuage*, during which the bottles, which have been placed horizontally on the *pupitres* (adjustable racks) are slowly moved from a horizontal position to a vertical one, cork downwards, to allow the dregs to slip down and rest on the cork. The sediment then has to be removed, and to this end the neck of the bottle is placed in a solution which freezes it. A lump of ice forms which encloses the sediment. The person in charge of this operation, which is known as the *dégorgement*, then removes the cork, and the pressure inside the bottle expels the ice and with it the sediment. Into the empty space he pours some *liqueur d'expédition*, which is a solution made from old champagne and sugar. This is known as the *dosage*, and whether the champagne becomes brut, sec, demi-sec or sweet depends on the proportions of champagne and sugar used. Only the type known as *extra brut dosage zéro* requires no *liqueur d'expédition* at all. A permanent cork is inserted and held in place with a solid mesh of wire and the champagne is ready.

The length of time for which it is allowed to age depends upon whether or not it is a vintage champagne. When the champagne is sold it is ready for drinking, and does not really improve by being stored in a cellar at home. It can, nevertheless, be stored for four or five years in a cool darkened place. The bottles should be kept in a horizontal position so that the wine is in contact with the cork. Champagne should be served cool but not iced, at a temperature around 6–8°C (43–46°F). The ideal glass for champagne is a flute with a long slender stem, which allows the bubbles to rise slowly to the surface in long streams.

Chartreuse

The origins of this spirit, distilled from herbs, are uncertain. It is thought that the inventor may have been a 16th-century alchemist, who made careful studies of plants and herbs (he listed 130 varieties in a manuscript, exactly the number needed to produce Chartreuse). In 1605 Marshal François d'Estrées decided to give this precious manuscript with the names of all the plants to the Carthusian monks of Vauvert. Nothing more was heard of it for more than a century, and then, in 1737, the same manuscript appeared at the Grande Chartreuse (the famous monastery situated in the foothills of the Alps, in Savoy). Here it was carefully studied, with the idea that it might be possible to produce a substance with strong medicinal properties. It was not until 1764, however, that a definitive document was compiled which led to the production of *Elixir de la Santé* and *Elixir de la Table* (the equivalent of green chartreuse). Gradually, a new version of the liqueur was developed, yellow chartreuse, which is a sweet drink. The Carthusian monks were by now producing three liqueurs: elixir, chartreuse verte and chartreuse jaune.

The recipes have remained almost unchanged right up to the present day. The soaking and ageing processes take place in huge oak casks in the cellars of the Voiron distillery. Towards the end of the period of maturation alcohol derived from wine is added to the drink, as well as alpine flowers and natural honey. After a few months the drink is bottled and exported world-wide. A certain percentage of the total amount produced is allowed to mature for a longer period, after which it becomes Chartreuse VEP (vieillissement exceptionellement prolongé). Both types of chartreuse are suitable as aperitifs or as ingredients for cocktails and long drinks. They can also be used in cordon bleu cooking.

Cherry brandy
This is another very old drink, whose origins give rise to a certain amount of controversy. It is made from a mixture of two spirits, distilled from wine and marasca cherries (which come from Dalmatia) and a syrup made from the same cherries. After the cherries have been stoned and crushed their juice is placed in round oak butts where it is allowed to stand until all the sediment collects at the bottom. The clear juice is then mixed with old brandy and sugar syrup, and it is then aged in oak casks. After a certain time the mixture is filtered and bottled. Cherry brandy is produced in many European countries (Italy, Holland, France, Denmark and Yugoslavia). The eventual sweetness of the drink depends on the quality of the cherries used and the exact way in which the liqueur, which is usually ruby red in colour, is made. There is a particular variety made in Denmark, with a lower alcoholic content, which is called cherry wine.

Cherry Heering
This is a type of cherry brandy made by the Heering Company of Copenhagen, following an exclusive recipe. The cherries used in making the liqueur are grown by the company especially for this purpose. Cherry Heering can be drunk as an after-dinner drink or as an aperitif, and is also used in the preparation of many cocktails.

Citron water
This is an Italian product, made by several specialist firms. It was very popular during the first decades of this century.

Coffee
The coffee plant comes originally from Caffa, a province in Ethiopia, but it was first used by the Arabs, who called it *qahwah*. The Turks pronounced this *qahve*, and their version gave the English coffee, the Italian *caffè*, the French and Spanish *café* and the German *Kaffee*. The Arabs, who drink great quantities of coffee, were also the first (at Mecca) to open public places especially for drinking it. Others soon appeared all over the world; places where friends could meet for a few minutes' relaxation. The first European coffee shop was opened in Venice in the 17th century.
If allowed to grow naturally, the coffee plant will grow as high as 8 metres, and produces an ovoid-shaped fruit (similar to a cherry). Beneath the flesh are two nuts and inside each of these is a seed covered with a thin silvery skin with a well-developed horny albumen and a small embryo. The latter is the coffee bean. The height at which coffee is grown varies: it grows in Brazil at 200 m (650 ft) above sea level, and at 2,200 m (7,200 ft) in the mountains of Venezuela. It is its ability to adapt to almost any terrain which accounts for its wide diffusion.
There is much discussion about the ideal way of making coffee, and many claim to have discovered the perfect formula. For Turkish coffee the coffee is boiled with the water, for Venetian coffee the ground coffee is passed through the water, in Neapolitan coffee the water passes through the coffee. Coffee machines (or those based on the hydrocompressant principle) work by rapid filtration of the water at 100°C (212°F) through the ground coffee which is pressed into a filter. The main coffee-consuming countries are Sweden, Finland, Denmark, Norway, Holland and Switzerland. Britain is not a large consumer: less than 3 kg (6½ lb) per head is consumed here each year. Coffee, of course, contains caffeine, which is an alkaloid much used in medicine for its stimulating effect on the cerebral cortex, on the nervous system, and on the heart.

Cognac
Cognac was first known in the region of Charente as early as the 16th century. The region is divided into seven wine-producing areas: Bon Bois, Grande Champagne, Petite Champagne, Borderies, Fins Bois, Bois Ordinaires and Bois Communs. The climate and the soil of the regions in which the vines permitted to be used are grown are, of course, important factors in determining the quality of cognac. But so, too, is the strictly controlled, old-fashioned method of production. Double distillation, using a copper pot still and naked flame, is still carried out in the Charente distillery. First, the wine is

poured into the boiler (which is bulb-shaped with a hood above), and a moderate heat is applied to bring the liquid to the boil. The alcoholic vapour which is given off gathers in the hood, runs into a special pipe, and condenses. This liquid is then placed in the boiler a second time. This *bonne chauffe* (final boiling) is a very delicate operation and calls for great expertise. The head (first vapour) has to be discarded, as does the tail, and only the heart of the distillate which contains all the characteristics of cognac is kept.

Once the distillation is complete, the cognac has to rest for a number of years in casks made of Limousin forest oak which gives cognac its amber colour and special aroma. After the ageing process, brandies of different years, and made from different vines, are blended together to ensure a harmonious and uniform product. It is the responsibility of the master of the cellar to perform this task, to examine the appearance of the cognac, its colour, smell and taste, and to blend it accordingly in such a way as to obtain the best possible result. It is then ready for bottling.

Cognac may be drunk in several different ways. Connoisseurs prefer it on its own after a meal, in classic brandy balloons which are held in the palm of the hand to encourage the cognac to release its subtle, unmistakable bouquet. It can also be used to make thirst-quenching long drinks in the summer months – cognac and soda is becoming increasingly popular. It serves as an excellent base for all types of hot drinks in the winter and, of course, it is used in many different cocktails to which it lends its characteristic delicate bouquet. Taken in small quantities it is particularly suitable for people with heart and circulatory trouble, as it has a vasodilatory effect as well as being an analgesic.

Cointreau

Cointreau originated in France in 1849 in the famous distillery at Angers which was owned by two brothers, Edouard and Adolphe Cointreau. The recipe calls for two distillations, during which process orange peel is soaked in alcohol. To ensure the high standard of the final produce, each time the liquid is distilled the head and the tail are discarded, and only the heart is retained. Finally, water, sugar and other ingredients are added. Cointreau is excellent drunk on its own or with ice, and it is also an essential ingredient in many cocktails. It is also very useful in cooking, adding a special touch to many excellent dishes.

Crème de bananes

This liqueur is yellow in colour, rather dense, and has a distinctive flavour.

Crème de cacao

Crème de cacao is a traditional sweet liqueur, made by distilling a mixture of various types of cocoa, alcohol and sugar. There are two varieties: white, which is sweeter, and clear, like water; and dark brown, which tastes stronger and slightly bitter, as a part of the ground cocoa still remains.

Crème de cassis

This comes from the area around Dijon. It is made by distilling blackcurrants and is deep purple in colour.

Crème de menthe

Crème de menthe is a liqueur made from a concentrate of mint leaves, and is available in a white and a green form. It is used particularly in the preparation of a large number of cocktails and long drinks, although it can also be drunk straight, with finely crushed ice.

Curaçao

This drink belongs to the family of sweet liqueurs, and is flavoured with the flowers and the skin of the bitter wild oranges from the island of the same name. There are various types of curaçao: white or triple sec, which is colourless and clear; orange, which is amber in colour and not as strongly alcoholic; green, yellow, red, and blue – all very vividly coloured – are much used in mixed drinks and sweets.

Drambuie

The name Drambuie comes from the Gaelic words *andram buideach*, meaning the drink which satisfies. The origins of this liqueur, which is made from old Scotch whiskies, heather honey and aromatic herbs, go back more than two centuries, to the time when Bonnie Prince Charlie, who had taken refuge on the Isle of Skye after being soundly beaten by the English troops, obtained the recipe for this liqueur from a member of the Mackinnon family. The Mackinnon family continued to produce Drambuie generation after generation and it soon became widely known and enjoyed, first in England, and later on the Continent. Drambuie is usually drunk neat, but it can also be drunk on the rocks, with a slice of lemon. It is used quite often in the preparation of cocktails.

Dubonnet

In 1846 in Paris, Joseph Dubonnet started to sell a new fortified wine which had the properties of a tonic and stimulant. Dubonnet soon became popular as an aperitif and is now known all over the world. It is produced in the Roussillon region of France from red mistelle, a maceration of crushed whole black grapes which is infused for a month so that all the nutrients, flavour and colour are preserved. The mistelle is pressed and then matured in oak vats. White mistelles from white grapes are also made. Both red and white mistelles are blended with fully matured Roussillon wines and further matured. The distinctive flavour of Dubonnet is obtained by infusion with aromatic herbs, flowers, roots and barks such as cinchona. Dubonnet is a completely natural product and takes up to two years to produce. It can be drunk neat, chilled or with a mixer added to taste. It is widely used in the preparation of cocktails and long drinks, especially those with a vodka or gin base.

Framboise
A spirit distilled from raspberries, without the addition of sugar, colourants or flavourings.

Galliano
On the morning of 8 December 1895 the Italian troops under the command of Major Giuseppe Galliano, who had been sent to defend the fort of Enda Jesus, near the ancient city of Makalle, in Ethiopia, were surrounded and decimated by 80,000 Abyssinians, commanded by Menelik, nephew of the Ethiopian Emperor, Haile Selassie. Although they were decimated, the courage of the Italian troops was praised throughout the whole of Italy. Arturo Vaccari, born in Tuscany, who owned a spirit factory, decided to name a new product of his after Galliano as a sign of his admiration of the commander's bravery. Galliano, whose fame quickly spread throughout the world, is composed of more than eighty ingredients, including herbs, roots, flowers and berries, most of which come from Alpine regions. The ingredients are infused in a hydro-alcoholic solution and distilled with other natural ingredients. The recipe is a carefully guarded secret, and the method of production has remained unchanged since Arturo Vaccari first instituted it.

Gin
Gin originated in Holland around the year 1600, when Franciscus de la Boe, a professor of medicine at the University of Leiden, decided in the course of his search for a substance with medicinal properties, to distil a mixture of alcohol and juniper berries. This drink soon became the national drink of the Low Countries, and from there passed to England. It was the English who made it so widely known, through their colonial expansionism and their maritime and commercial links with the rest of the world.
Since those days the methods of production have changed, with the result that the gin made today is much drier than it used to be. There are two main methods of production. Distilled gin is obtained by distilling juniper berries and other substances; mixed gin is made by infusing juniper berries and other substances to provide flavouring, in neutral alcohol. According to which combination of substances is used (and it should be remembered that as well as juniper berries and alcohol many other kinds of aromatic herbs such as coriander and roots such as angelica are used) gins with different tastes are obtained.
The best known gins available are: *Dutch gin* (jenever) which is made in Holland, and which differs from the other varieties in that a mixture of rye and germinating barley is fermented along with the juniper berries; *London dry gin*, perhaps the most widely-consumed gin in the world; *Old Tom*, which is produced exclusively in Britain and is less popular, having a noticeably sweeter taste due to the addition of sugar; *Plymouth gin*, which lies between London dry and Old Tom, being neither very dry nor very sweet; and *Golden gin*, so-called on account of its colour, which is mainly due to the fact that it is matured in oak casks.
There is also a large number of flavoured gins: orange gin, lemon gin and sloe gin, flavoured with sloe berries. The latter varieties, which have a lower alcohol content than the others, are becoming quite popular. Gin can be drunk neat, on the rocks, and it is also used as an ingredient in many famous cocktails and long drinks.

Ginger ale
A non-alcoholic effervescent drink made from an essence of the aromatic herb ginger, sugar and carbonated water, it is available in sweet or dry forms. It is used on its own as a soft drink or to dilute the alcoholic base of drink, such as whisky (especially bourbon).

Grenadine
This non-alcoholic syrup, known the world over and popular with adults and children, is made from pomegranates. Barmen and connoisseurs of cocktails in particular recognise in it the ideal complement to many cocktails and it is used in a great many long drinks. As well as its strong flavour, it lends to these drinks a

bright colour which enlivens even the most colourless of substances, such as vodka and white rum. Care should be taken in its use, however. As it is very concentrated, a few drops will usually suffice; to use more is to run the risk of completely changing the characteristics of the drink in preparation. Since it is very sweet, a small amount will obviate the need to add sugar. Grenadine is also used in cookery, especially in desserts.

Grand Marnier
A liqueur composed exclusively of old champagne cognac combined with bitter oranges. It is particularly suitable as an after-dinner drink, and is widely used in cocktails, ice cream, desserts and in cordon bleu cookery.

Grappa
The origins of grappa have never been pinned down to a specific period of time nor to a particular region of Italy. Even the name grappa has been attributed to different roots, some people claiming that it comes from the word used in the Friuli region of Italy *sghapa* (which in turn derives from the German *schnapps* meaning spirits), while others believe it comes from the Venetian word *graspa* (*graspo* in Venetian dialect means either a bunch or a grape-stalk). Grappa is made by distilling either selected pressed grapes, or the solid parts of the skins, pips and stalks which remain after pressing for wine. This reddish mass is technically waste material, but can still yield an excellent end product.
It makes sense that grappa should be produced in the area where the ingredients are grown because, when distilling grappa, it is necessary to have access to a distillery where the production cycle can be completed before the month of December, thus avoiding having to store the pressed grapes in silos for long periods, which causes a certain loss of aroma. There are two main types of grappa, Piedmontese, made with wine from the best grapes of the Piedmonte region (such as barolo and moscato d'asti); and those from the regions of the Veneto, Friuli and Trento.
Starting from sometimes imperfect methods of distillation, such as the direct flame and bain-marie methods, techniques have gradually been improved, so that the product now obtained is purer and of a much higher quality. The distillation of grappa takes place in the following way: the dregs of the pressed grapes are placed in stills, and steam is introduced under low pressure. The steam heats up the pressed grapes, causing them to release their alcoholic vapour which rises to the top of the still. This vapour is guided into a second still, where the whole process is repeated, and where the vapour is enriched with alcohol. When the vapour reaches the top of the second still it is immersed in the distillation column where it reaches a high concentration. It then passes into the condenser and from there to the refrigerator.
Once the 'head' and 'tail' have been discarded, the product can be called grappa. To make the Veneto variety of grappa, merlot, prosecco or raboso grapes are used, the variety the experts call neutral to distinguish them from those with a stronger aroma and taste, such as vernaccia. The technique of distillation now used, known as the steam method, has remained more or less the same for some time, except that the pips and stalks are not always used, allowing a more delicately flavoured product to be obtained. Grappa which is to be allowed to age is placed in oak casks, where it remains for at least three years, gaining colour and aroma.
Today, various grappas of different quality are available in the shops: *stravecchia, alla ruta* (very old, with the traditional twig in the bottle), *cristallo* (clear), and others obtained by adding different ingredients (honey, orange, etc). There are also varieties which contain no methyl alcohol, or almost none. When drunk on its own, grappa should be served in small narrow glasses, but it is being used more and more as an ingredient in after-dinner cocktails.

Irish whiskey
Irish whiskey is made using a mixture of malted and unmalted barleys, and, by law, must be allowed to age for at least five years. However, most distilleries allow their product a minimum of seven years, and some much longer. Whiskey is left to age and mature in special selected oak casks in storerooms where the temperature is controlled. These are watched over by technicians whose expertise is handed down from one generation to the next. Some people claim that the Irish developed the art of making whiskey before anyone else, possibly after the missionary monks brought the secret of distilling to Ireland around 500–600 AD. Around 1170, after the first invasion of Ireland by the English, it was introduced into England where it became very popular. By the 18th century the fame of Irish whiskey had travelled far, reaching even the court of the Russian Tsar, Peter the Great.

Jack Daniel's whiskey
This very distinctive brand of American whiskey is produced in the Hollow distillery in Tennessee, using a special procedure (known as charcoal mellowing) introduced by the founder of the distillery, Jack Daniel, around 1866. Hollow is ideally situated for the production of whiskey because it has a natural spring, providing a source of fresh water, at a temperature which remains constantly cool all the year round. This water contains no iron, a fact which is most important, for even a small amount can do irreparable harm to the whiskey. The Hollow water is used to cool the whiskey mixture, which is contained in vats two storeys high, built directly in the course of the water. The water is thus used as a substitute for the air-conditioning which is used to cool distillates where there is no natural spring.
In the hills around Tennessee, near Hollow, grows a tree called the wood maple. Many years before Daniel's day a black slave had the idea of filtering whiskey through charcoal derived from the maple. This process lent a slightly smokey flavour to the whiskey which had the effect of ageing it. Jack Daniel remembered this experiment and repeated it on a much larger scale in his distillery. He discovered, what is more, that the hard maple which grows on the hills around Hollow is, in fact, the wood best suited for this type of charcoal filtering, so charcoal mellowing, gave a local flavour to the whiskey he produced. The tree is cut down when it is tall and mature, then stacked in a special way and set alight. Care must be taken at this stage that it does not dissolve into ashes. The charcoal thus obtained is collected and taken to the charcoal mellowing room where it is placed at the bottom of the vats to a depth of about 3 m (12 ft). At this point the whiskey is poured slowly into the vats, and drips slowly out, smooth and refined.

Kirsch
This pure white cherry brandy is distilled chiefly in Germany, Alsace and Switzerland from the fermented juice of small, black and very juicy cherries which grow in a wild state in the Black Forest and other mountain areas.

Mandarinetto
An Italian liqueur made principally from the famous Sicilian mandarin oranges. It is used to add colour and flavour to cocktails and long drinks.

Maraschino
The story of maraschino, from its birth as cherries to its completion as a liqueur, involves several stages which embrace the various technical procedures by which fruit is transformed into spirit. The Euganean Hills (in the Veneto region of Italy) is one area where many of the small cherries, picked in June and sent to the distilleries, are grown. At the distillery the first process is to remove the stones from the ripe fruit. The fruit is then pressed and the *torte* (cakes) thus obtained (so named because of their shape) are collected and stored. They are then placed in large vats made from larch, where they are allowed to stand in a distillate made from cherry stones. This initial ageing process continues for several months. The infusion is passed repeatedly over heat and is then poured, refined and purified, into casks and vats made of ash where it remains for several years. During this period, the product, and especially the bouquet, improves further, and the drink is then exported world-wide.
In the case of Luxardo maraschino, the cycle is not yet complete; the distillate is mixed with pure sugar syrup and then allowed to stand for several months in large oval casks made from ash. When it is removed from these it is filtered, so that it becomes crystal-clear, and bottled in characteristic straw flasks.

Martini
A brand of vermouth produced by a very old Piedmontese firm. It is made in three varieties: red, white and dry (see vermouth).

Orange bitter
A bitter (that is, a highly alcoholic drink which has the properties of a tonic, and can be drunk before or after a meal) made from the peel of bitter Seville oranges. It is used in small quantities to add flavour to mixed drinks (cocktails and long drinks).

Peach bitters
A liqueur obtained by distilling an infusion of wine and peaches.

Pernod
This French aniseed-flavoured liqueur has an elaborate and secret recipe. Fourteen plants, including melissa, parsley, camomile, coriander, veronica and spinach, are macerated in alcohol then this extract is blended with anise essence. This highly concentrated essence is, in turn, blended with very pure alcohol of vegetable origin, plus a little sugar and distilled water. Pernod is usually served mixed with water as an aperitif, but it is also thirst-quenching when diluted with orange, lemon or grapefruit juice and served with lots of ice, or it can

provide the spirit base for a variety of cocktails.

Pimm's No 1 Cup
An English drink made from a jealously guarded original recipe which includes bitters, it is available in two forms – with gin and with vodka. A delightfully refreshing long drink, particularly suitable for serving in summertime, can easily be made by the simple addition of other substances such as three or four parts of lemonade, some cubes of ice, slices of lemon and cucumber.

Plants
Medicinal plants are used in a large number of alcoholic drinks, and an attempt is made to draw the maximum benefit from them. The use of plants and herbs is as old as man, and began when people saw how sick and injured animals instinctively turned to them, and tried to imitate this behaviour themselves. Many parts of plants can be used to make drinks, such as the fruit, berries, flowers, leaves, tip of the plant, bark, stem, roots, rhizome, bulb, seeds, or, sometimes, the whole plant. They are stored in cool, dry, airy places, or may be kept in hermetically sealed boxes. Let us now take a closer look at the plants which are particularly useful in making alcoholic drinks.
One form of *achillea* grows in mountainous regions, near the snow line. The essential oil extracted from this plant is used to make several liqueurs, including the Swiss drink, Iva. Ground *almonds* are often distilled at the same time as the fruit pulp in the manufacture of liqueurs. From the leaves of the *aloe* plant a highly valued, bitter-tasting liquid is obtained, which is used to make fernet. *Alpine mugwort* is a highly prized little plant, used in the preparation of drinks with particularly delicate flavours and bouquets. *Angelica* has aromatic and therapeutic qualities for which it has been used in herbal medicine since antiquity. It is now used particularly in the production of vermouth. The *angostura* is a tree which grows on the banks of the Venezuelan river Orinoco, whose bitter-tasting aromatic bark is used in the production of various drinks, and especially of bitter liqueurs and tonics. *Anise* is widely used in a variety of different liqueurs (such as centerbe and fernet), and in its pure state it can be used to modify other drinks, including non-alcoholic ones. Distilled water and essential oil are extracted from *balm mint* for use in medicines and alcoholic drinks. The bark of the *bergamot* tree is crushed to obtain an oil which is used in various drinks. *Cinchona bark*, with its slightly bitter taste, is very widely used in the preparation of alcoholic drinks, especially bitters. The bark of the *cinnamon* tree produces an oil of the same name which is used to make perfume and medicines as well as many drinks, such as fernet, centerbe, gin and vermouth. *Cloves*, which are in fact the dried flowers from a tree which originated on the Moluccas Islands, have long been used as a spice, on account of their piquant and aromatic properties. They are also used in certain drinks, of which centerbe is one. *Cocoa* beans, reddish-purple in colour, and with a pleasant smell and slightly bitter taste are used in the preparation of drinks as well as in cookery. *Coriander*, a plant which originated in the East, produces fruit the size of peppercorns which are used as a flavouring in a number of different drinks, including fernet. *Gentian* leaves can be used, or even the whole plants, including the roots. The rhizome of the *ginger* plant, a herbaceous plant from which a drug is obtained, is yet another source of an essential oil frequently used in the production of alcoholic drinks. The fruit of the *hop*, yellowish, bitter, but pleasant, is indispensable in the making of beer. *Juniper* berries, black in colour and rich in sugar and oils, are used in the preparation of gin. *Lemon* skin contains a very important essential oil which is widely used in the preparation of drinks. *Mint* leaves, which should be picked when the plant is in flower, are also widely used in drinks. *Musk mallow*, a plant which originated in India, is useful particularly for its small brown seeds. *Nutmegs*, which are obtained from a large tree found in the wild in the Philippines, contain an essential oil which is used in the preparation of centerbe. There are some twenty varieties of *rhubarb*, the best known undoubtedly being the Chinese variety, which is valuable as a tonic, and much used in alcoholic drinks. When distilled in steam *rosemary* produces a limpid colourless oil which, like the aromatic herb *sage* is also used in drinks. The roots of the *valerian* plant, which grows in shady spots near running water, are particularly useful in making medicines and alcoholic drinks. The fruit of the *vanilla* plant, which originated in Mexico but is also grown in Java and Madagascar, is usually sold as small, dark sticks with a pleasant smell, and is frequently used in making sweets and cakes as well as drinks. *Wormwood* – a plant with clusters of small yellow flowers, which contains a bitter substance and a volatile oil. The most important of its substances

used in pharmacology is the essential oil, which has a powerful effect on the nerve centres. This is the same oil as that used in the preparation of fernet and vermouth.

Poire William
This is a pear liqueur, well-known in France, Switzerland, Germany and Italy, made from William pears. It has a strong aroma and a very delicate flavour.

Port
The companies which produce port are all situated near the town of Vila Nova de Gaia, opposite Oporto, on the banks of the river Douro. This river flows from Spain into Portugal and crosses the border at the town called Barca d'Alva. It then continues through the Douro district and flows into the Atlantic at a point level with Oporto. The extent of the Douro district has been defined by Portuguese law and consists of an area which varies between 30 km (13½ miles) and 60 km (37 miles) in width, and is approximately 100 km (62 miles) in length from the frontier town of Barca d'Alva to a precise point situated to the west. This is the only area in the world where port may be produced.
The harvesting of the grapes is a ritual, begun by the women who do the actual picking, placing the grapes in enormous baskets which the men then carry on their shoulders to the deep stone jars which are known as *lagares*. They are then crushed and the must is stirred constantly for eight hours, with a pause in between of two hours. As soon as this phase is over the must begins to ferment, and the longer it is allowed to ferment the drier the wine will eventually be. Some of the must is poured into great wooden barrels (*tonels*) and some is poured into casks. In both cases it is at this point that alcohol is added (in the form of a distillate made from surplus Portuguese wine), in order to arrest the fermentation while there is still sugar in the wine and to preserve its natural sweetness. The wine is then poured into casks and barrels and sent to Vila Nova de Gaia where it is stored while awaiting exportation. On arrival there the wine is carefully tasted and classified according to its bouquet and quality. Eventually the wines are blended, to harmonise the aroma.
Port can be red or white although there is no difference in the method of production used. It depends merely upon whether black or white grapes are used. When red port is young it is dark in colour and full and fruity in taste, but the longer it is kept in the casks, the lighter its colour becomes and the more delicate its taste and bouquet. The styles available are full red, ruby, tawny, and old tawny. White ports, however, darken with age, and there are different styles available, varying in hue and dryness. Especially noteworthy is vintage port, for which high quality wine and maturation are indispensable. When there is a particularly good harvest in the Douro area, a limited amount of wine from that one year is chosen and placed in casks for a few years to rest. It is then sent to Oporto, where it is bottled directly. In this way vintage port, unlike other types of port, ages actually in the bottle.

Royal Stock brandy
This Italian brandy, made in the Stock distilleries in Trieste, is allowed to mature for more than three years. Although it only appeared on the market in 1968, it has won unanimous praise for the care and accuracy which go into its preparation and for first class blending.

Rum
Rum is a spirit produced from the fermentation and distillation of sugar cane in cane-growing countries. Sugar cane was introduced to the Caribbean islands by Christopher Columbus and, by the 16th century, was being distilled there into rum. In the next hundred years this highly aromatic spirit became well established in South and North America and Europe for medicinal use and as a cheering social drink. There are three main types of rum, although many rums are blends. Fermentation of the molasses may take only two days for white rums, which are distilled by the continuous process; several days for the golden, medium styles; and perhaps two weeks for the dark rums which are made in traditional pot stills. Rums shipped to the United Kingdom, from the West indies and South America, have, by law, to mature for a minimum of two years, which they do in oak barrels previously used for bourbon. After this, they are blended, 'married' in fresh barrels for another six months, then bottled. Rum can be served straight, or mixed in classic cocktails or exotic long drinks. It also makes a wonderful winter drink served hot, either neat or in a toddy.

Rye Whiskey
Rye whiskies are produced in both the United States and Canada by distilling a mixture of cereals; in the United States, the mash must by law contain at least 51% rye. The colour of rye is the same as that of bourbon, but its taste and aroma are decidedly stronger.

Sambuca
An Italian liqueur made from anise, to which suitably prepared herbs and roots are added.

Scotch whisky
The first historical record of Scotch whisky appears in the Exchequer Rolls of 1494 but, greatly valued, 'the water of life' was being distilled several centuries before this date. Government attempts to impose tax on whisky and generally control its production were much resented by the Scots who took to clandestine distillation and smuggling with a fierce fervour – 'Freedom and Whisky gang thegither!' wrote Robbie Burns. It was not until the early 19th century that the highland distillers began to legalize their business and organise it on a commercial basis. The development of blending in the 1860s produced a smoother spirit, which was acceptable to the English and became famous throughout the world. There are now over 100 distilleries in operation, each producing a whisky with a distinctive taste.
No one quite knows what gives Scotch whiskies their distinctive and inimitable taste. It seems to result from a combination of the distilling process, essential oils in the malted barley, the local waters, the peat which is burnt to dry the malt, and the effects of the Scottish climate on the maturation of the whisky.
There are two basic kinds of Scotch. Malt whisky is made from malted barley only by the old pot still process, has a stronger 'smokier' flavour and aroma, and takes longer to mature. Grain whisky is made from malted barley, together with unmalted barley and other cereals, by the continuous, patent (Coffrey) still process. Malt whiskies come from four areas – the Highlands, Campbeltown, Islay and the Lowlands – and vary from the heaviest Islay whiskies to the lighter Lowland ones, while grain whiskies may be distilled anywhere. The individual whisky from each distillery may be sold as a single whisky, but most are used to produce a huge variety of blends.
Whisky making is divided into five stages. *Malting* The barley is soaked, then spread on the malting floor to germinate. As this happens the barley secretes the enzyme diastase which makes the starch in the grains soluble, ready for conversion to sugar. Germination is halted by drying. *Mashing* The dried malt is ground to grist and mixed with hot water so that the soluble starch turns into a sugary liquid, wort, which is drawn off and cooled. *Fermentation* While it is in large vessels, living yeast is added to the wort and attacks the sugar which becomes crude alcohol. *Distillation* The alcoholic liquid wash is heated so that it vapourises. The spirit produced is monitored so just that of an acceptable standard is collected. *Maturation* The new spirit is stored in oak casks so that it mellows – perhaps taking fifteen years or longer. Only then is it ready to be drunk or skilfully blended.
Scotch is extremely versatile. It can be savoured neat; served as a hot toddy, or on the rocks; diluted with spring water, soda or dry ginger; and, of course, it provides the basis for many well-known cocktails.

Sherry
In Spain, between the Guadalquivir and the Guadalete rivers, there is a region, more or less triangular in shape, of nearly 15,000 hectares (over 40,000 acres), which is entirely given over to vineyards. This is the region famous for the production of sherry. Its main cities are Jerez de la Frontera, Puerto de Santa Maria, and Sanlucar de Barrameda. The vines need attention at two different times in the year: first in autumn, when the ground has to be prepared so that the winter rain can penetrate deep into the earth; and secondly in the spring and late summer, when weeding is necessary. The harvest begins at the end of August and the beginning of September, and is celebrated with a week-long fiesta. After they have been picked, the bunches of grapes are laid out on mats in the sun to increase their sugar content. After the pressing, the must is taken into the *bodegas* (large underground cellars), where the first stage of the fermentation takes place. During the second stage, which lasts about ten weeks, all the sugar contained in the must is transformed into alcohol, producing a very dry wine. The sweeter sherries are obtained by adding brandy to the grape juice, or by adding *dulce* (must which has been collected in casts containing brandy) which does not favour fermentation, and which retains the natural sweetness of the must.
The fermented dry wines are ready by early spring, when they are drawn of the dregs and left in casks which contain only the wine of one particular year. Even when the must comes from the same vineyard, the contents of each cask will probably be different from the next, at the end of the maturation period. This is how the light *fino* sherry, the full-bodied *amontillado* and the smooth *oloroso* first appear. The individual

types of sherry that have now emerged are collected into *oriaderas* – groups of casks of individual sherries which are placed one above the other in three rows, with the oldest wine on the bottom. The sherries are then poured from one cask to another, the bottom-most casks receiving younger wine from those higher up.
The colour of the matured and blended sherry varies from pale yellow, through amber and golden, to dark brown. The main varieties are: *manzanilla*, which is light yellow and very dry; *fino* which is fruity and not quite as pale (it is always served well chilled); *amontillado*, which is amber, and has an aroma vaguely reminiscent of hazelnuts; *oloroso* is dark golden, mellow and slightly sweeter with a tang of walnuts; *cream* is sweet and smooth. The different sherries can be served as aperitifs, dessert wines, liqueurs; on the rocks with, perhaps, a dash of soda; or used in cocktails.

Slivovitz
This dry and bitter tasting spirit is made by distilling a variety of small plums which are grown in the Danube basin and countries such as Austria, Hungary, Yugoslavia, and Italy (Friuli and Alto Adige).

Soda water
The taking of naturally sparkling mineral waters was thought to be good for the health, but they were difficult to obtain. This inspired a Swiss jeweller, Jacob Schweppes, to experiment with a carbonation system and, in 1783, he sold his first bottle of Schweppes aerated water. Nowadays, soda water (which contains sodium bicarbonate and carbonated water) is a vital ingredient in both long drinks and short cocktails.

Spumante
The main characteristic of sparkling wine is that it froths – due to the development of gas (carbon dioxide) – when the bottle is opened and the wine poured out. There are two different types of *spumante*: a natural one in which the carbon dioxide results from the fermentation of sugar, and one to which the gas is added artificially. The latter *spumante* bears the label *vino addizionato in anidride carbonica* (wine to which carbon dioxide has been added). Natural *spumante* is more highly regarded because of its superior quality and its production is closely supervised and strictly legislated. The traditional method of producing *spumante* consists of allowing the wine to ferment in bottles (when it becomes carbonated) followed by a long ageing period without the removal of the yeast which brought about the carbonation. The different stages of the natural process during which the wine becomes *spumante* are: bottling, carbonation, maturation, tilting of the bottles while still in their supports, then uncorking.
To make the wine ferment, yeast must be added, as well as the substance which enables it to act. This may be cane-sugar or sugar-beet. The yeast, plays an important part in ensuring that the final product is of a high quality. It must be active at low temperatures (the temperature in places where the bottles are stacked up for fermentation to take place is normally 11–13°C (52–55°F). It must also be able to cope with the pressure from the carbon dioxide which it produces, and it must give off a pleasing smell and as little volatile acid as possible. Finally it must form a sandy or chalky deposit which, rather than sticking to the bottle, can easily be removed from it. Together with the wine base, the yeast is undoubtedly the most important factor in determining the quality of the final product.
The wine is now ready to be bottled in traditional champagne bottles, where it will remain until it is ready to be drunk. The cork used is a temporary one (nowadays corona caps are considered both practical and functional) and it is replaced with the permanent cork after several years when the process is completed. When the new corks have been put in position, the bottles are stacked horizontally in cool dark cellars, where the temperature is kept constant all the year round at about 11–13°C (52–55°F). During the next six months the yeast causes the sugar to ferment, and the carbon dioxide is slowly released and dissolves into the wine. This means that when the wine is poured out it will produce a froth consisting of a great number of tiny bubbles. Once the fermentation which takes place in the bottle is complete, the wine can be called *spumante*, but the yeast must remain in contact with the wine for a further two to three years, so that the substances which have been removed from the wine during the reaction with the yeast can be returned to it. The only intervention necessary during this period of maturation is to re-stack the bottles every six months. The object of this laborious task is to remove any bottles which might be broken, and by shaking the bottles to place the deposit formed by the fermentation in suspension in the liquid once more. When the periods of fermentation and maturation are over the *spumante* has assumed its characteristic taste and

smell, and the process of eliminating the dregs can begin. The bottles are placed in special supports, and with an expert flick of the wrist, they are turned through an eighth of a circle every day. After careful checking the bottles are removed from the racks and held with the cork facing downwards ready for the extraction of the sediment. The next stage requires a certain degree of skill, and the person who carries it out also needs to be an experienced wine taster. So that as little pressure as possible is lost, the wines are placed in a refrigerator and cooled to around 0°C (32°F), after which the neck of the bottle is placed in brine at −25°C (−13°F), so that the small amount of wine near the cork in which the dregs are contained, freezes. The bottle can then be placed in a normal upright position without the sediment dispersing throughout the *spumante*, and the bottle can be uncorked. The anchor of the corona cap is removed, and pressure between the wine and the ice causes the ice to shoot out of the bottle violently taking the sediment with it. The bottle is then placed in a machine which replenishes the amount lost with an exact quantity of syrup composed of refined cane sugar, old wine, and possibly a small quantity of good brandy or fortified wine. According to how much of these are added, the wine will be more or less sweet, and will be called natural, extra-dry, brut, sec or demi-sec. After being topped up in this way, the wine is ready for its permanent cork, which is wired on. All the necessary procedures have now been completed, and all that remains is to store the wine for a few months while the liqueur and the wine marry together.

As well as this classic method in which the wine ferments in the bottle, there are two other ways of making *spumante*, whereby the wine is placed in large closed vats to ferment and re-ferment using the continuous system. The first of these methods, known as the Charmat method, was initially developed to cut down on the amount of time and money necessary to produce *spumante* by the classic method. It is particularly successful when used to make wines whose original taste does not need to be changed, and which can therefore benefit by retaining the fullness of their original flavours and the freshness of their smell. The second way is based on refermentation, and uses a carefully judged amount of active yeast which is allowed to accumulate in special containers. This method generally produces a superior *spumante*.

Sugar

This substance is vital to the preparation of cocktails. The alcohol in drinks is formed by the fermentation of some form of sugar, either that derived from the original material – grapes or grain, for example – or that added at some stage of manufacture. Also, sugar can be added to sweeten the final product, or caramelised sugar can be added to deepen its colour. When cocktails are mixed sugar is often added – as lump sugar, as a plain syrup made by dissolving with boiling water, or as part of fruit syrups or liqueurs.

Sucrose – the sugar which we buy and which is generally used as an additive – is obtained from both the roots of sugar beet and the stems of sugar cane. The latter, which was the original source of sugar, probably came from Polynesia several thousand years ago. Its use spread gradually through India to China, then Persia, then to the eastern Mediterranean. From the seventh century conquering Arabs introduced the plant and process of extraction to North Africa and southern Spain. In the 11th century returning crusaders brought back Syrian sugar which they sold for very high prices and by the 14th century Levantine sugar was being processed in Venice and exported to England. When Europeans began settling in the New World they took sugar cane with them and great fortunes were made from the huge plantations that were established in the favourable climate of the Caribbean sea.

With such plentiful supplies no one tried to perfect the extraction of sugar from beet until the French ports were blockaded during the Napoleonic Wars. A French chemist then succeeded in refining it commercially and by 1880 home-grown beet had taken over from cane as Europe's principal source of sugar. Britain, however, continued to use her colonial sources of cane and it wasn't until 1925 that the sugar beet industry started expanding until, now, a third of all the sugar we consume is produced here.

Swedish punch

This nordic drink, produced primarily in Sweden, is a cordial with rum as its basis. It is highly spiced and may be drunk neat as a liqueur or used in cocktails.

Syrups

There are many syrups on the market in every country in the world. The ingredients used in their preparation include fruit juices (strawberry, raspberry, orange, mandarin, etc), extracts of aromatic herbs (mint, etc), roots, rind or grains (tamarind, barley-water, etc), and sugar syrup (liquidised sugar to which water is added). Syrups are normally served with the addition of water or soda as thirst-quenching drinks, or in cocktails and long drinks, either to add colour or to make the drink sweeter.

Tea
Nobody knows when tea was first used as a drink, but it may well have been around 2500 BC in the south of China where tea bushes grow wild. Its use gradually spread to many countries until, in 1649, the first cargo of Chinese tea reached Holland, and by 1657 the drink was being served in a London coffee house. Tea was such a success with the English that, although it was an expensive luxury, by 1750 it was the principal drink of all classes.
The British have continued with their passion for tea. It accounts for half of everything we drink, and Britain imports more tea than any other country in the world. Our imports come mainly from India, Kenya and Sri Lanka. In general, when blended, north Indian teas (especially those from Assam) provide strength; Sri Lankan and south Indian teas provide flavour; and African teas provide colour. Green teas and aromatic black teas are imported in small quantities from China and Japan.
The tea bush is an evergreen tropical plant with stiff shiny pointed leaves which grows up to an altitude of 2100 m (7000 ft) – the higher slopes producing finer teas – and likes a warm, wet climate. Only the leaf bud plus the top two leaves of the soft growing shoots are plucked. These go to the tea estate factory where, to get the black tea usually drunk in Britain, they are withered, rolled, fermented and dried.
The main substances which determine the characteristic taste of tea and produce the relaxing, reviving qualities are caffeine (1–4.5%), tannin (5–26%), essential oils (0.6–1%) and mineral salts (3–8%). The varying quantities in which these substances are present depend on the time when the tea was picked and the altitude and climatic conditions of the plantation.
The French were the first to add milk to their tea in about 1680 and this is still how it is usually drunk in Britain. However, served with lemon instead, either hot or iced, it makes a refreshing long drink, as iced minted tea, and it can be included in long mixed drinks.

Tequila
This is a spirit obtained by fermenting and then distilling the sap of the agave plant which is a member of the Amaryllis family. Tequila is the national drink of Mexico where considerable quantities of it are consumed, as wine is not considered a suitable accompaniment to meals. The alcoholic content varies between 40° and 45°, and its flavour is unique. It is usually drunk very cold, in a curious ritualistic way, accompanied by a pinch of salt and a slice of lemon. The glass is held in one hand and the slice of lemon and the salt are placed on the back of the other.

Triple Sec
A sweet liqueur with an orangy taste (see curaçao).

Tonic water
Indian quinine or tonic water, containing quinine whose bitterness was first tempered with sugar then masked with lemon or lime and gin, was originally drunk as a preventative against fevers, particularly malaria. The quinine content is no longer sufficient for medicinal purposes but provides a refreshing flavour and tonic water is usually used to dilute spirits such as gin or vodka, but can be drunk on its own with ice and a slice of lemon.

Vermouth
Vermouth is not a liqueur but a fortified wine flavoured with herbs and other substances. Its name is derived from the best known of the plants used in its production, the *arthemisia absintium* or wormwood (*Wermouth* in German), a herbaceous plant with a woody root, which has a bitter taste and a volatile oil. The flower is used in wine and liqueur often producing excellent results, as is the case with vermouth. Vermouth, which is the pride of the Italian wine-producing industry, is a typical product of the Piedmont region. It first appeared as early as 1786, and a few pioneers had enough vision to see the potential of the new product, not only at home, but also abroad. It was first introduced to France, a country well versed in glamourising high-quality products and launching them amid a blaze of publicity. Production began, at first hesitantly, in a wide area around Turin, and gradually spread to the surrounding regions, rapidly increasing the international fame of the drink. The volume of substances added to the drink should not exceed 30% of the finished product, which should be clear. These substances are added altogether in the form of an alcoholic infusion made up from ingredients including bark (cinnamon, Peruvian bark, etc); flowers (camomile, cloves, hops, saffron, etc); leaves and complete

plants (wormwood, thistles, dittany, hyssop, marjoram, balm, sage, etc); fruit (anise, orange, cardamom, coriander, mace, nutmeg, vanilla, etc); roots (angelica, sweet flag, gentian, ginger, syrup of aloes, etc). As well as these ingredients a sufficient quantity of alcohol is, of course, needed. It is clear that obtaining these herbs and plants, which come, as the list above suggests, from all over the world, is one of the most difficult tasks necessary for the production of vermouth. Another important task is the blending of wines from different regions and the addition of the muscat wine obtained from top-quality grapes grown in the most famous vineyards. This latter procedure is not always used these days. There has recently been a change in the way vermouth is produced. Previously all the herbs and plants were placed in a special container and immersed in the wine during the infusion stage. This rather primitive system has now been abandoned for economic reasons, and has been superseded by a modern process which allows the aromatic elements to dissolve into the wine more effectively. The choice of the herbs and plants and the correct combination, taking into consideration their quality, and how much of each should be used, and finally blending and infusing them, are all very delicate and complex operations which require considerable expertise and a great deal of time. After the preliminary stages of preparation there is a purification stage when all impurities are eliminated. The next stage is refrigeration, followed by filtering, which is repeated several times for maximum efficiency, and bottling, using bottles of different sizes to suit the different foreign markets. The ageing process which varies in length according to the type of vermouth and the demands of the market, is the final stage, and is also very important to the success of the product. A good vermouth should not be too strongly alcoholic, ould not greatly exceed the minimum gradation laid down by the law. It should not have a very strong bouquet nor be too bitter. The perfect marrying of the taste and perfume of the plants and herbs with those of the wine is achieved by first leaving the mixture in a refrigerator for a long period, and then exposing it to heat so that it becomes biologically stable and is at the same time pasteurised. The wine for sweet vermouth has sugar added to it, and the wine used to make the red variety is coloured with burnt sugar. The first type of vermouth to be produced commercially was the red variety. It is a dark amber colour and is known as Italian Vermouth or sometimes even Turin Vermouth, leaving no doubt as to its exact origin. The next variety to appear was sweet vermouth (*bianco*) with its distinctive straw colour. *Dry* vermouth usually has a higher alcoholic gradation but a lower sugar content. The *chinciti* variety (with Peruvian bark added) is rather bitter, and tends only to appeal to the connoisseur, and for this reason it is sold and produced in smaller quantities. The colour of this type is more definite than that of the classic *red* variety, which has a sugar content of at least 19%, the highest of all the types of vermouth. Another variety is *americano* vermouth, which suits modern tastes. To make this, several ingredients normally associated with the preparation of bitters are used (eg Peruvian bark rhubarb, angelica, gentian). Finally, there is also vermouth *rosé*, made with top quality wine. Its colour is bright pink, its bouquet is very subtle and its taste very light, all of which account for its delicate colour and aroma. In order to be sure that it will remain perfectly stable, vermouth *rosé* needs to undergo certain processes before being bottled: these are pasteurisation, refrigeration and filtration. At the end of these processes, the vermouth is allowed to rest in tanks and casks for a prescribed length of time, so that it reaches the shops in perfect condition.

Vodka

Vodka, the most typical and best-known Russian drink is so old that some people claim that it goes back as far as the Tsar Peter the Great. To be fair, however, it must be stated that this spirit is also distilled in almost all the countries of Northern Europe including Poland. Russian vodka is made from alcohol made with pure maize, which then undergoes special treatment and is filtered through active charcoal from the birch. As well as the classic colourless vodkas (all with an alcoholic gradation of 40°, i.e. *Moskovskaya* which is one of the best dry vodkas), *Stolichnaya*, *Kristal* and *Russkaya* (which differs from the first variety in that it is more mellow), there are also the coloured varieties. The colourants used are all natural products, and consist of lemon skin for *Limonnaya* vodka, an infusion of aromatic herbs and leaves from Crimean apple and pear trees for *Starka* and *Okhotnichya* (known as Hunters' vodka, with an alcoholic gradation of 45°) and hot peppers for the famous *Pertsovka* which is amongst the least alcoholic (35°).

Finally, there is also a variety called *Krepkaya*, which is the most alcoholic (56°) and which is used mostly in cocktails. Polish vodka, on the other hand, is made with rye, which is rectified twice, and then left to age before being submitted to further processes, including filtering. The best known varieties are *Wjborowa*, with a delicate bouquet and an alcoholic gradation of about 45°; *Jerzebiak*, strongly aromatic, with an alcoholic gradation of 40°; *Wisniowka*, made from a base of scented cherries (40°); *Zubrowka*, to which aromatic herbs are added (40°); *Zytnia*, which is the most classic vodka (40°); *Starka*, which has a higher alcoholic gradation than the Russian vodka of the same name (50°); *Krakus*, which has a very delicate flavour and an alcoholic gradation of about 40°. Wherever the vodka may have been made, and whatever its taste and aroma, it is always served well chilled in cold glasses.

Water
Water is used in large quantities in the preparation of drinks, and tap water is usually adequate. However, if the water supply is particularly hard or the chlorine content very evident, it is worth using bottled spring water. Carbonated water is used to manufacture mixers (such as soda water and tonic water) which are used in the preparation of long drinks and, with the addition of fruit flavouring, is the base for branded lemonade, bitter lemon and other fruit drinks. Water, of course, also has a solid state: ice. The importance of ice both in the preparation of a cocktail (when it is used in the shaker or mixing glass) and also to cool a long drink, has already been stressed. Ice should be crystal-clear and free from sediment. In order to achieve this, and to ensure a light, neutral taste, it may be worth making it from bottled spring water.

Worcestershire sauce
Famous English sauce produced at Worcester, which contains vinegar, molasses, sugar, shallots, essence of old and matured anchovies, tamarinds, soya, pepper, salt and garlic.

Balloon A special glass used for cognac or brandy.
Crusta A type of cocktail served in a glass with its rim encrusted with sugar.
Cup A type of long drink which is prepared in a large bowl or carafe and which is served well chilled. Usually it has a wine base.
Fizz A long drink, usually consisting of lemon juice, an alcoholic substance (such as gin) and soda water.
Flip A drink to which a fresh egg is added.
Flute A special glass for serving champagne and spumante.
Frappé Used to describe a liqueur when it is served on crushed ice.
Grog A hot drink, usually with an alcoholic base.
Highball Belongs to the category of long drinks, and has a fizzy substance among its ingredients. The glass in which it is served has the same name, which it acquired from the American habit of referring to whisky with ice and soda as a highball.
Long drink A mixed drink which is served cold. Usually fruit juice and sparkling wine or other fizzy substances are added to an alcoholic base, giving a low alcohol content.
Mixing glass A glass for the preparation of cocktails. The ingredients are poured in then stirred with a long-handled spoon.
Old Fashioned A short tumbler, like a whisky tumbler.
Pillé Crushed ice; having been finely chopped, the *pillé* ice is placed into glasses, into which the alcoholic mixture is poured.
Pousse café A cocktail prepared in a tall narrow glass. The different liquids to be used are poured in one at a time, beginning with the most dense and viscous so that they do not mix. Thus different coloured bands can be obtained.
Punch This drink was invented by the English in the 18th century, during the time of their rule in India. It is said that to combat the constant thirst which they experienced in that country, the English prepared a drink composed of five elements: arrack (a highly alcoholic substance), tea, sugar, water and lemon juice. Now punch is made more simply with water, sugar, lemon and rum or a liqueur made from mandarins or orange. Sometimes in the winter, despite the use to which the drink was originally put, it is drunk hot.
Sangria A drink which originated in Spain, made with a base of wine. It is made in a carafe or large container with red wine and slices of orange and lemon, and flavoured with cinnamon and cloves.
Shaker This is a special closed container which is used for mixing together the various components of a cocktail.
Short drink The true 'cocktail', which is highly alcoholic.
Zombie A drink which belongs to the long drinks category, although it is highly alcoholic. It is characterized by the large number of ingredients from which it is made and it is served in 285 ml ($\frac{1}{2}$ pt) glasses.

Index

Page numbers in italics refer to illustrations.